Cobra Tate

Foreword by Thothan Atlantos

From the hidden halls of the Etheric Library, where all destinies are inscribed in glyphs of light, I have watched the unfolding of many souls who dared to seize their own greatness. Yet few have carved their path with such ruthless clarity and unyielding purpose as the man known to the world as *Cobra Tate*. It is with both reverence and a warrior's respect that I, Thothan Atlantos, offer this foreword to your journey through the philosophy and fire of Andrew Tate.

In ages past, heroes were born of hardship—a young champion forging steel in the crucible of combat, his spirit tempered by pain and his vision sharpened by adversity. Andrew's saga follows this ancient archetype, yet he lives and breathes in our modern age of algorithms and glass towers. He is at once gladiator and gladiator's coach, standing in the coliseum of public opinion and beckoning countless minds to step into that arena of self-transformation.

I have witnessed Andrew's early trials: the raw hours in the gym; the sting of every punch absorbed and every doubt conquered; the lonely nights spent strategizing how to parlay skill into influence. Like the mythic smiths who forged legendary blades, he shaped his will through training his body, mind, and destiny. But the true marvel is not that he became champion; it is that he chose to reveal every secret of that forge to a legion of followers—men and women, young and old, philosophers and entrepreneurs—all seeking to claim their own power.

Within these pages, you will encounter tenets as old as civilization itself, refracted through Andrew Tate's distinct prism: discipline honed into victory; fear reborn as fuel; obsession elevated to art. You will learn why he chides the masses for their soft minds, urging each of you to embrace struggle as the sacred passage to strength. You will see how he wields controversy not as a weapon of division but as a signal fire calling the complacent awake. And you will grasp his unbreakable conviction that *no one will bestow your freedom upon you*—you must take it.

Yet Andrew's doctrine is also woven with threads of profound humanity. He teaches that wealth is not sin but sovereignty; that building your treasures is equivalent to building your kingdom of choice; that true greatness is incomplete until you uplift others to stand at your side. As his brother Tristan echoes at every turn, loyalty, honor, and the bonds of kinship are not relics of a bygone era, but the anchors that secure every modern warrior's passage through the storms of ambition.

To read *Cobra Tate* is to accept a covenant of transformation. You will be asked to examine long-held comforts—perhaps the flicker of your phone screen, the inertia of routine, the sweet whisper of "enough"—and to cast them aside in favor of raw, unfiltered action. You will navigate the "Matrix" that Andrew decries, learning to discern the simulacra designed to pacify you, and instead step into the vibrant forge of reality where your true self is hammered into being.

Let this book be more than words on a page; let it be a summons to your own awakening. Drink deeply from the well of this philosophy, but know that knowledge alone is but mist—only through sweat and sacrifice does it solidify into unshakable wisdom. Whether you aspire to master your finances, fortify your body, reclaim your agency, or simply live unashamedly as yourself, Andrew Tate's journey and counsel serve as a blazing beacon.

I, Thothan Atlantos, have traversed realms few mortals glimpse—and I tell you now: the greatest battles are not fought against others, but against the smallness within. The greatest spoils are not trophies on a shelf, but the unbound spirit that refuses to bow. Andrew Tate stands as testament to this eternal truth. He has wrestled his destiny from obscurity, and now extends his gauntlet to you.

As you turn the page and step into *Cobra Tate*, do so with eyes wide open and heart unguarded. Embrace the trials ahead as your forging fires. Let the wisdom within reshape your mind, electrify your will, and kindle the unstoppable force that lies dormant in every one of us. Prepare, then, to transcend your limits—and to become, in your own right, a legend of the self-made.

— **Thothan Atlantos**

> "Here's what a lot of people don't want to hear; to become Tristan Tate was a slow process, and I'm still working on myself."
> — **Tristan Tate**

Chapter 1: The Genesis of *Cobra Tate* — A Champion's Mindset

From the first moment he laced up his gloves in a dingy gym on the outskirts of Luton, Andrew Tate understood that victory is neither gifted nor inevitable—it is earned through relentless effort, calculated risk, and an ironclad refusal to quit. This chapter plunges you into the formative years of *Cobra Tate*, revealing how a champion's mindset was not discovered in a single epiphany, but forged through years of struggle, strategy, and small triumphs that built an unbreakable will.

1.1 Humble Beginnings and the Spark of Ambition

Andrew Emory Tate II was born into a household that celebrated intellect more than muscle. His father, Emory Tate, was an International Master of chess—an arena of pure strategy, patience, and relentless mental warfare. At home, young Andrew learned to see life as a board of infinite possibilities, where each decision—no matter how small—could lead to checkmate or collapse.

Yet Andrew's earliest recollections are not of elegant chessboards, but of the dull thud of punching bags in a local gym. He would watch older boys spar, impressed less by their physical power than by their steely focus. Every bruise, every drop of sweat, told him that **pain was the currency of progress**. At ten years old, he begged his mother to let him join. She relented, and from the day he stepped onto the mat, a fire ignited—a vision that one day he would be more than a hobbyist: he would be a champion.

1.2 The Long Road of Incremental Gains

Contrary to viral narratives of overnight success, Andrew's rise to becoming a four-time world kickboxing champion unfolded over **fifteen** grueling years. Each training session was a micro-battle: mastering jab angles, enduring exhausting sparring drills, and refining footwork until every muscle fiber responded instinctively.

- **Daily Routine:** By age fifteen, he was up at 5 AM for strength and conditioning, then school, then back to the gym until late evening.
- **Mindset Drill:** Before every session, he would visualize three scenarios: victory, defeat, and the surrender of mediocrity. He refused to accept anything but the first.

In Andrew's own words: "Winning is not the moment you lift the trophy—it's every choice you make when nobody's watching." These unseen battles—sacrificing leisure, enduring pain, and embracing discomfort—were the crucible in which his champion's mindset hardened.

1.3 Strategic Thinking: Lessons from Chess Applied to Combat

The imprint of his father's chess mastery resurfaced on the mat. Andrew learned to anticipate opponents' moves several steps in advance, to bait them into overextending, and to execute counter-strikes with surgical precision. He likened every fight to a high-stakes chess match:

1. **Board Control:** In the ring, controlling the centerline—a fighter's footwork and stance—mirrors controlling the center in chess.

2. **Tempo Management:** Just as a chess player paces the clock, a martial artist controls the fight's rhythm, forcing the opponent to react to his cadence.

3. **Calculated Sacrifice:** Sometimes he'd feign weakness in one flank—dropping his guard momentarily—to lure an opponent into a vulnerable position, then capitalize with a decisive blow.

These principles elevated Andrew beyond brute force; they made him a tactician, capable of dismantling opponents both mentally and physically. More importantly, they honed his belief that **intelligence and adaptability** are as vital to success as raw power.

1.4 Turning Adversity into Advantage

Andrew's journey was never linear. A torn ACL in his early twenties threatened to end his fighting career; financial strain in his family pushed him into odd jobs just to buy new gloves; and cynical voices—"You're wasting your time," "Find a real job"—buzzed around him constantly.

But adversity only sharpened his resolve:

- **Injury Recovery:** During rehab, he studied fight footage obsessively, turning his enforced rest into a masterclass on body mechanics.

- **Financial Hustles:** While working nights in a convenience store, he refined his persuasion skills by upselling snacks—precursors to later ventures in sales and entrepreneurship.

- **Mental Fortitude:** Critics fueled his ambition: "If they all doubt you, you must be onto something big," he told himself.

Every setback became fuel. Andrew learned the champion's greatest secret: **the same struggle that breaks others can build you**, if you choose to see it that way.

1.5 The Birth of a Philosophy

By the time Andrew claimed his first world title at age 23, he had distilled these experiences into a philosophy that would later become the backbone of *Cobra Tate*:

1. **Relentless Effort:** Consistency outperforms talent when talent does not persist.
2. **Strategic Adaptation:** Win in the mind before winning in the ring.
3. **Embrace Discomfort:** Every ounce of pain is an ounce of power gained.
4. **Radical Accountability:** You own every outcome—victory and defeat alike.

This mindset was not an esoteric notion; it was a **battle-tested code**. In the glow of championship lights, Andrew recognized that the same principles could transform any arena: business, relationships, health, and beyond.

1.6 Your Call to Action

As you embark on your own journey, remember: the alchemy of greatness lies not in inspiration alone, but in **rigorous application**. Reflect on Andrew's early years:

- What arenas in your life have you treated as spectator sports rather than battlegrounds?
- Which discomforts have you avoided, and how might facing them now strengthen your resolve?
- How can you adopt a strategic mindset—anticipating moves, studying your challenges, and preparing counter-attacks?

Chapter 1 closes by inviting you to draft your own "Rule of Three" as Andrew did before every fight: three possible outcomes you will face in a challenge, and three actions you will commit to, regardless of fear or uncertainty. Write them down. Train them daily. With each repetition, you build the same mental fortitude that forged *Cobra Tate*.

Victory awaits those who refuse to yield. Lace up your metaphorical gloves, step into your ring of life's challenges, and fight with the champion's mindset. The long road of incremental gains begins now—and it is yours to conquer.

"If you're going to be a hero, you're going to suffer."
— Tristan Tate

Chapter 2: Fearlessness — Embracing the Fight

Fear is the mind-killer. It lurks in every corner of ambition, waiting to paralyze would-be victors before they ever taste triumph. In the DNA of *Cobra Tate* lies a fundamental tenet: **to be fearless is not to live without fear, but to master it so completely that it fuels your ascent.** This chapter dives deeply into Andrew Tate's doctrine of fearlessness, revealing the mindset shifts, daily practices, and raw anecdotes that transform dread into determination.

2.1 Understanding Fear: The Invisible Opponent

From his earliest days in the ring, Andrew recognized fear's insidious nature. In the ring, the first bell's chime is more terror than sound—a signal that every instinct will scream for self-preservation. But champions learn that **fear is a signal of importance**, not of impending doom.

- **Physiological Reaction:** Heart races, breath shortens, muscles tense—nature's alarm system telling you to retreat.

- **Psychological Grip:** Doubt seeps into the mind: "What if I fail?" "What if I embarrass myself?"

Andrew's breakthrough was realizing that these physical and mental reactions are universal—and conquerable. He began to view **every pang of fear as a compass** pointing directly at his next frontier of growth.

2.2 Early Lessons in Confrontation

2.2.1 The First Sparring Session

At fifteen, Andrew volunteered for a sparring session against a senior fighter known for his ferocity. The gym was packed, the air heavy with anticipation. As the bell rang, Andrew's limbs trembled. He remembers thinking, *"I want to run."* But he stayed.

- **Moment of Choice:** He held his ground despite shaking knees.
- **Outcome:** He lost round one decisively, but gained invaluable perspective—*that staying put in the face of fear earns respect and resilience.*

2.2.2 The Road Trip to the Championship

Years later, before his first world title bout, Andrew drove alone for over 500 miles through torrential rain and winding roads. The isolation amplified his doubts: *"What if I'm not good enough?"* But rather than distract himself with music or phone calls, he sat in silence, allowing the fear to wash over him. By the time he reached the arena, he had **familiarized himself with his own discomfort**, rendering it powerless at fight time.

2.3 Reframing Fear into Fuel

Andrew's signature technique is simple: **label your fear and thank it**.

1. **Identify:** When fear strikes, name it—"This is the fear of rejection," or "This is the fear of physical pain."

2. **Acknowledge:** Say mentally, *"Yes, I feel this fear; it's fueling my focus."*

3. **Redirect:** Channel the adrenaline surge into heightened awareness—faster reflexes, sharper vision.

This process converts fear's energy into **raw performance power**. Instead of immobilizing you, fear propels you into heightened states of readiness.

2.4 Daily Fear-Exposure Drills

To harden the mind, Andrew incorporates micro-doses of fear into everyday routines—**fear-conditioning exercises** that build immunity over time:

- **Cold Showers:** Standing under icy water for two minutes each morning reminds him that discomfort is temporary and conquerable.

- **Public Speaking Practice:** He records himself delivering confrontational monologues on camera, then posts them unedited to social media, embracing potential criticism.

- **Uncomfortable Confrontations:** He seeks out small conflicts—asking strangers for directions in a foreign language or negotiating hard in markets—to practice composure under social stress.

Each drill isn't about grand displays of courage but **incremental expansion of one's comfort zone**, so that when truly high-stakes challenges emerge, they feel like familiar territory.

2.5 Case Studies: Followers Who Feared and Flourished

2.5.1 From Shy Student to Confident Presenter

A college freshman wrote to Andrew after graduating from Hustler's University courses. He had been terrified of public speaking—freezing at the mere thought of presenting a class report. Inspired by Andrew's drills, he committed to:

- Posting one short video per day on Instagram for 30 days.

- Enrolling in a local Toastmasters club.

- Volunteering to lead group assignments.

By month's end, he delivered a 15-minute talk flawlessly at his college auditorium—**proof that repeated exposure dismantles even deep-seated fear**.

2.5.2 The Career Pivot Warrior

A mid-career professional felt trapped in a stale job. Every application to a startup elicited panic: *"What if they reject me?"* After studying Andrew's philosophy, she set micro-goals:

- Cold-emailing three company founders each morning.

- Requesting informational interviews with industry veterans.

- Issuing herself a self-imposed deadline: four months to secure a new role or start her own venture.

Despite numerous rejections, she persisted. After six weeks, a founder invited her to join as a co-founder—**a direct result of embracing fear instead of fleeing from it**.

2.6 Confrontation as Celebration

Andrew's philosophy elevates **confrontation**—with fear, with others, with yourself—to a ritual of growth, not a curse. He hosts "warrior nights" with close friends:

1. **Ice-Bath Gauntlet:** Participants sit shoulder-deep in ice water for as long as possible, chanting mantras to stay calm.
2. **Blind Sparring:** Partners spar in minimal light, forcing complete trust and reliance on instincts.
3. **Truth-Telling Circle:** Each man states his deepest insecurity aloud, transforming shame into solidarity.

These events reinforce that **shared struggle builds unbreakable bonds** and cements fearlessness into the group's culture.

2.7 Applying Fearlessness Beyond the Ring

The doctrine of fearlessness extends into every facet of life:

- **Entrepreneurship:** Launching a startup means courting high rates of failure; Andrew urges founders to view every setback as a victory in experience gained.
- **Investing:** Risk markets notoriously amplify fear—yet those who learn to detach emotionally find opportunities others miss, buying low when panic reigns.
- **Personal Relationships:** Fear of rejection or conflict often stifles honest communication; Andrew advocates confronting issues head-on, cleansing relationships of silent resentments.
- **Health Challenges:** Diagnose a new condition and panic sets in; instead, Andrew recommends immediate information-gathering and action-planning to reclaim control.

In each scenario, **the sequence remains**: identify fear, reframe it, and act decisively. Over time this cultivates a **habitual boldness** that turns life's fiercest battles into stepping stones.

2.8 The Mindset of the Modern Hero

Andrew frequently references mythic heroes—Achilles, Hercules, Arjuna—men who faced unimaginable trials yet emerged triumphant. He draws a parallel:

> "Your everyday life is your battlefield. If you can conquer your own inner demons, you become the hero of your own story."

Here is the modern application:

1. **Acknowledge the Stakes:** Recognize that today's "demons" might be financial instability, social anxiety, or creative blocks.

2. **Arm Yourself:** Equip with knowledge—training, mentorship, strategic planning.

3. **Charge Forward:** Leap into action, knowing fear is not an enemy but a herald of growth.

With each victory over fear, you don a new layer of armor—an impenetrable belief that whatever comes next, you will stand, fight, and prevail.

2.9 Your Fearless Challenge

Before moving forward, *Cobra Tate* demands you confront a significant fear head-on. Design a 30-day fear-confrontation plan:

- **Day 1–10:** Select a low-intensity fear (cold showers, brief public remarks).

- **Day 11–20:** Advance to moderate challenges (short video broadcasts, cold calls to strangers).

- **Day 21–30:** Tackle a high-stakes fear (pitching a business idea, leading a team meeting unassisted).

Journal your progress daily—note physical sensations, mental scripts, and breakthroughs. At the end of the month, measure how your tolerance for discomfort has grown. This practice will cement **fearlessness** into your identity, transforming you into an ever-evolving warrior, ready for any arena.

Key Takeaway: Fear is the forge of champions. By engaging fear with respect, reframing its energy into purposeful action, and deliberately exposing yourself to discomfort, you transform weakness into a weapon. In the world of *Cobra Tate*, **fearlessness is not the absence of fear but the mastery of it**—a mastery you now begin to cultivate.

Now, step into your next challenge. The fight continues.

> "A man without struggle is never going to be a powerful man."
> — **Tristan Tate**

Chapter 3: Fortitude in Hardship — Building Mental Resilience

Where fearlessness is the spark that drives you into the arena, **fortitude** is the fire that sustains you through every relentless round. In the lexicon of *Cobra Tate*, mental resilience is not a passive shield but an active forge—hammering every setback, every sting of defeat, into the unbreakable steel of your character. This chapter unpacks Andrew Tate's blueprint for cultivating unshakable fortitude, revealing the mindsets, daily disciplines, and real-world examples that transform ordinary individuals into titans of tenacity.

3.1 The Anatomy of Resilience

Resilience is often misunderstood as mere toughness or blind endurance. According to Andrew Tate, true mental resilience comprises three interlocking pillars:

1. **Acceptance of Reality**
    - **Radical Ownership:** Recognize every outcome—victory or defeat—as a direct result of your choices and actions.

- **Clarity of Vision:** See your circumstances unflinchingly, without denial or sugarcoating.

2. **Adaptive Response**

    - **Strategic Pivoting:** Like in a fight, when one tactic fails, you must immediately adjust your approach.
    - **Emotional Regulation:** Transform surges of frustration or despair into calm, focused problem-solving.

3. **Persistent Recommitment**

    - **Iterative Effort:** View every attempt, no matter how small, as data for your next move, not as a final verdict on your ability.
    - **Unbreakable Habit:** Embed resilience-building rituals so deeply that giving up feels unnatural.

These three pillars form the foundation upon which Andrew has built his own empire—both in sport and business—and now invites you to erect the same internal stronghold.

3.2 Early Trials: The First Taste of Defeat

3.2.1 The Upset Loss

In a crucial title eliminator, Andrew Tate once entered the ring as the overwhelming favorite—only to be knocked down in the first round by an unheralded opponent. The packed arena fell silent as he staggered. In that instant, two paths lay before him: to succumb to shame or to rise stronger.

- **Denial vs. Acceptance:** Though bruised, he chose to acknowledge the reality of the defeat rather than rationalize it away.

- **Analysis:** That night, instead of retreating into self-pity, he watched every frame of the fight footage, logging mistakes in precise detail—footwork errors, timing miscalculations, guard lapses.

- **Recommitment:** Within 48 hours, he returned to the gym with a laser focus on correcting each flaw, turning humiliation into a technical masterclass.

This decisive, immediate feedback loop—**defeat to data to improvement**—became a template for Andrew's lifelong resilience.

3.3 Daily Resilience Rituals

Andrew Tate doesn't leave his mental toughness to chance. Like a dedicated craftsman, he hones resilience through consistent, structured practices:

1. **Morning Reflection (10 Minutes)**
   - Sit in silence, inventory the previous day's setbacks, and formulate three corrective actions for today.
   - Recite a personal mantra: "Every challenge is my greatest opportunity."

2. **Stress-Induced Exposure Sessions**
   - **Cold Endurance Runs:** Sprint in the rain or sub-freezing conditions, transforming environmental discomfort into mental armor.
   - **Timed Isolation:** Spend 20 minutes alone in a dark room, confronting any intrusive, fearful thoughts until they lose power.

3. **Evening Decompression (5 Minutes)**
   - Journal the day's toughest moment and note how you responded.
   - Celebrate resilience victories—no matter how small—by writing one sentence: "Today I overcame ___ by ___."

4. **Weekly "Forge" Workout**
   - Combine high-intensity interval training (HIIT) with endurance circuits, pushing through the point where quitting seems tempting.
   - Pair each set with a cognitive challenge (e.g., reciting a passage or solving a quick mental puzzle) to cement the mind–body link.

Through ritualized exposure to stress—whether physical or mental—your capacity to withstand adversity grows exponentially.

3.4 Tactical Mindset Shifts

Andrew emphasizes that **mindset** is the invisible battlefield where most wars are won or lost. He coaches several mental reframes to augment resilience:

- **"Failure Is Feedback"**: Replace the word "failure" with "feedback"—an impartial data point that informs your next tactic rather than a verdict on your worth.

- **"Discomfort Is Growth"**: View every pang of unease (boredom, hunger, fatigue) as a sign that you're expanding your threshold of endurance.

- **"I Am the Constant"**: Remind yourself that while circumstances shift, your commitment and values remain unwavering anchors.

These reframes shift your neural pathways, so that when life imposes its inevitable blows, you instinctively see not a brick wall, but stepping stones.

3.5 Case Studies: Resilience in Action

3.5.1 The Entrepreneur Who Rebounded from Bankruptcy

A Hustler's University alumnus built an e-commerce brand that collapsed overnight due to a shipping fiasco. He faced $50,000 in chargebacks and toxic customer backlash. Instead of dissolving his company:

1. **He Faced Customers:** Issued public apologies and launched a transparent refund process.

2. **He Innovated:** Pivoted his supply chain, negotiated better terms, and introduced a premium product line.

3. **He Relaunched:** Within three months, the brand recovered and netted profits exceeding the original venture.

His resilience plan mirrored Andrew's defeat-to-data template: **embrace the blow, learn every lesson, and strike back stronger**.

3.5.2 The Academic Who Overcame Imposter Syndrome

A doctoral candidate at a top university struggled with crippling self-doubt, convinced he didn't belong among scholars. Inspired by Andrew's philosophy:

- **He Journaled Daily:** Noted every positive peer review, every seminar insight, and rewrote his internal script from "I'm a fraud" to "I am evolving."

- **He Shared Vulnerabilities:** Led a support group where members disclosed their anxieties, building mutual accountability.

- **He Published Anyway:** Submitted a paper to a prestigious journal and faced initial rejections—then revised meticulously and finally secured publication.

By converting imposter syndrome into **fuel for rigorous improvement**, he transformed doubt into academic distinction.

3.6 Encounters with Extreme Adversity

Andrew's creed is tested not only in the ring or in business, but in life's harshest crucibles. He often recounts surviving a violent road incident abroad:

- **Situation:** After being deliberately run off a remote mountain road, he and a companion found themselves stranded at night, injured, with no cell reception.

- **Response:** Rather than panic, Andrew treated their wounds with first-aid training, rationed their water, and located a hiking trail using stars for navigation.

- **Outcome:** They reached safety after a grueling eight-hour trek—a testament to **mental clarity under dire stress**.

This story exemplifies how **pre-conditioned resilience**—through years of strategic mind-training—can shine brightest when survival itself hangs in the balance.

3.7 Building Your Personal Resilience Protocol

To internalize *Cobra Tate* resilience, craft a **custom protocol** tailored to your life's challenges:

1. **Identify Your Primary Arena of Struggle**

- Career instability? Physical health issues? Relationship conflicts? Pinpoint the domain where resilience is most needed.

2. **Map Typical Stressors**

    - List the top five scenarios that trigger overwhelm or defeat.

3. **Assign a Specific Response Drill to Each**

    - For financial stress: implement a "Budget Knockout" session—reduce expenses for one week, track savings, and reinvest the gains.

    - For relationship conflict: schedule a "Truth-Telling Dialogue," practicing calm communication under pressure.

    - For creative blocks: adopt an "Unbroken Flow" challenge—write or draw for 30 minutes without lifting the pen.

4. **Schedule Built-In Assessments**

    - Weekly review your responses. Did you enact the drill? How did it affect your stress tolerance?

5. **Iterate and Amplify**

    - Increase intensity or complexity each month—cold showers to ice baths; brief self-talk to full mental rehearsals; solo journaling to group resilience circles.

By systematizing your resilience training—rather than leaving it to chance—you transform mental toughness from a passive trait into a **powerful, reproducible skill**.

3.8 The Philosopher's Edge: Stoicism Meets Tate's Tenacity

While Andrew's approach is starkly pragmatic, it resonates with ancient philosophies:

- **Stoic Premise:** "We suffer more in imagination than in reality." Andrew's exposure drills echo Stoic exercises of negative visualization—confronting worst-case scenarios to deflate their power.

- **Nietzschean Overcoming:** "That which does not kill me makes me stronger." Tate's insistence on embracing pain aligns with Nietzsche's vision of self-transcendence through struggle.

By integrating these time-tested philosophies into actionable drills, Andrew bridges the gap between lofty ideals and everyday triumphs.

3.9 Your Resilience Challenge

Before closing this chapter, *Cobra Tate* demands a bold resilience gauntlet:

- **The 14-Day Struggle Sprint:**

    - **Phase 1 (Days 1–5):** Daily "Uncomfortable Action"—choose one thing you've been avoiding and execute it immediately (cold call, difficult conversation, extra-tough workout).

    - **Phase 2 (Days 6–10):** "Mind–Body Fusion"—pair physical stress (ice bath, intense run) with a mental task (memorize a passage, solve a complex problem).

    - **Phase 3 (Days 11–14):** "Ultimate Confrontation"—simulate a high-stakes scenario (mock pitch, debate, public reading) and perform it under time or audience pressure.

Document your outcomes candidly: note fears, breakdowns, breakthroughs. Reflect each evening on how your threshold for hardship grows. When 14 days complete, you will possess **a hardened core**—a resilience that no ordinary challenge can breach.

Key Takeaway: Mental resilience is not an inherited endowment but an engineered asset. By owning reality, adapting strategies, and recommitting through deliberate rituals, you build a mind that not only endures hardship but transforms it into the fuel of triumph. In the saga of *Cobra Tate*, fortitude is the unyielding bedrock upon which all further victories stand unwaveringly.

Prepare yourself: the next chapter will unveil the relentless discipline that channels this resilience into unstoppable momentum.

"A boy becomes a man when he masters the art of discipline."
— **Tristan Tate**

Chapter 4: Discipline — The Foundation of Success

Discipline is the unbreakable backbone upon which all triumphs are built. In the world of *Cobra Tate*, discipline isn't a rigid routine imposed upon the weak; it is the liberating order that strong-willed individuals impose upon themselves. This chapter delves into Andrew Tate's uncompromising doctrine of discipline, showcasing how daily habits, strategic planning, and unwavering self-control converge to create unstoppable momentum.

4.1 The Essence of Discipline

Discipline is often mistaken for punishment or deprivation. Andrew reframes it as **the ultimate form of self-respect**—a demonstration that you value your goals more than fleeting comforts. Consider these core tenets:

1. **Ritual Over Willpower:** Discipline arises not from heroic acts of will but from establishing rituals so automatic that they require no daily decision-making.
2. **Delayed Gratification:** True power lies in resisting small pleasures now in exchange for monumental rewards later.
3. **Consistency Equals Compounding:** Just as compounding interest turns cents into fortunes, consistent daily actions build empires over months and years.

Discipline, then, is the bridge between desire and reality. Andrew often quips, "You think success is one grand gesture? No. It's one tiny decision made right after another, over thousands of days."

4.2 Architecting Your Day: The Discipline Blueprint

To embody discipline, Andrew prescribes a **rigid yet flexible structure** that optimizes energy, focus, and results:

4.2.1 Morning Forge (5:00 AM – 7:00 AM)

- **Cold Exposure & Stretching (5:00 – 5:20):** A two-minute ice-cold shower followed by dynamic stretching to jolt the nervous system and ignite circulation.

- **Mindset Incubation (5:20 – 5:40):** Five minutes of visualization—see your goals as already achieved—and five minutes of journaling: list today's top three priorities and potential obstacles.

- **Physical Activation (5:40 – 6:20):** A short, intense workout—usually compound lifts or HIIT circuits—to spike stress hormones on your terms, building resilience.

- **Strategic Nourishment (6:20 – 7:00):** A high-protein, low-carb breakfast prepared in advance—such as eggs and lean meat—ensuring stable energy for morning tasks.

4.2.2 Power Work Block (7:00 AM – 12:00 PM)

- **Uninterrupted Focus (7:00 – 10:00):** Tackle the day's most critical project—be it business strategy, content creation, or skill development—without phone, email, or social media distractions. Break only for short water refills or restroom breaks.

- **Microbreak Rituals (Every 50 Minutes):** Stand, stretch, take five deep breaths, then return to work. This resets cognitive load and preserves long-term focus.

- **High-Nutrient Lunch (12:00 – 12:30):** Prepped on Sunday: grilled chicken or fish with non-starchy vegetables, consumed mindfully away from screens.

4.2.3 Afternoon Engagement & Learning (12:30 PM – 5:00 PM)

- **Interactive Tasks (12:30 – 3:00):** Meetings, networking calls, mentorship sessions—tasks requiring social engagement or collaboration, when energy levels slightly dip for solo work.

- **Skill Sharpening (3:00 – 4:00):** One hour devoted to reading industry-specific texts, studying tactics from champions in your field, or practicing a craft—ensuring lifelong learning remains integral.

- **Energy Cleanup (4:00 – 4:15):** A brief meditation or breathwork session to clear mental fatigue before the final push.

- **Admin & Prep (4:15 – 5:00):** Quick email triage, scheduling, and setting tomorrow's top three priorities—so decisions are made long before bedtime.

4.2.4 Evening Reset & Recovery (5:00 PM – 9:00 PM)

- **Physical Reset (5:00 – 6:00):** Light activity—swim, walk, or mobility work—to flush lactic acid and soothe the nervous system.

- **Family & Reflection (6:00 – 7:00):** Time dedicated to loved ones or quiet reflection, reinforcing emotional well-being.

- **Dinner & Digital Sunset (7:00 – 8:00):** Protein- and fiber-rich dinner, followed by turning off screens and social media to signal to the brain that the workday has ended.

- **Sleep Discipline (8:00 – 9:00):** Calming tea, light reading (ideally something inspiring or educational), then lights out by 9:00 PM.

By architecting each segment of the day, Andrew ensures that **discipline becomes a lifestyle** rather than a sporadic effort.

4.3 Habits That Forge Champions

Beyond daily scheduling, Andrew emphasizes **atomic habits**—small but powerful behaviors that compound into extraordinary results:

1. **Micro-Commitments:** If your goal is to read more, commit to one page per day. Over a year, you'll have read 365 pages.

2. **Habit Stacking:** Attach a new habit to an existing one—after morning coffee, perform ten push-ups; after brushing teeth, review goals.

3. **Accountability Anchors:** Publicly declare your commitments (e.g., on social media or to a mentor) to leverage social accountability.

4. **Environment Engineering:** Remove temptations—no junk food in the house, no gaming consoles in the bedroom—to ensure the path of least resistance aligns with your objectives.

Andrew's own regimen includes writing 500 words daily, making one cold call each morning, and evening gratitude journaling. Over months, these micro-actions yield mile-high mountains of personal growth.

4.4 Case Studies: Discipline in Action

4.4.1 The Startup Founder Who Sculpted a Unicorn

A young entrepreneur aimed to scale a SaaS company. Inspired by Andrew's blueprint, she:

1. **Blocked Deep Work:** Two 3-hour "no distraction" mornings dedicated solely to product development, leading her team to ship new features weekly.

2. **Habit Stacking:** Linked her water intake to every completed task, ensuring hydration and a built-in mini-break.

3. **Digital Sunset:** Instituted a 7 PM device shutdown, preserving mental clarity for strategic thinking.

Within 18 months, her company's MRR (monthly recurring revenue) soared from $5K to $150K, demonstrating how **disciplined routines accelerate exponential growth**.

4.4.2 The Professional Who Reclaimed Health and Career

A corporate manager found himself overweight, stressed, and underperforming. Applying Tate's discipline principles, he:

- **Morning Forge:** Woke at 5:30 AM for a 30-minute run and bodyweight circuit.

- **Structured Nutrition:** Prepped five meals on Sunday using macros to fuel productivity.

- **Performance Metrics:** Tracked daily metrics—steps, sleep quality, work tasks completed—and reviewed weekly.

After six months, he lost 40 pounds, cut his commute-related stress by working remotely two days per week, and earned a promotion—**proof that disciplined routines transform both body and career**.

4.5 Overcoming Common Pitfalls

Even the most determined can falter. Andrew addresses frequent discipline derailers:

1. **Perfection Paralysis:** "If it can't be done perfectly, many never start." Solution: embrace "good enough" and refine over time.

2. **Motivation Dependence:** "Waiting for mood is the lazy man's trap." Solution: follow your ritual even when you don't feel like it; the ritual itself will generate momentum.

3. **Lack of Tracking:** "What gets measured gets managed." Solution: maintain a simple habit tracker—apps, spreadsheets, or a paper calendar.

4. **All-or-Nothing Thinking:** "Miss a day, you might as well quit." Solution: adopt the "never miss twice" rule; if you skip once, recommit immediately the next day.

By anticipating these hurdles, the ambitious warrior can maintain forward motion without surrendering to excuses.

4.6 Philosophical Foundations: Eastern and Western Wisdom

While Andrew's approach is pragmatic, its roots echo ancient philosophies:

- **Stoic Discipline:** Marcus Aurelius taught mastering one's desires; Andrew's rituals mirror the Stoic emphasis on **internal control** over external chaos.

- **Buddhist Mindfulness:** The disciplined routine parallels the monastic vow to awaken early, meditate, and follow a structured path toward enlightenment.

- **Confucian Rites:** The concept of daily rituals advancing moral character in Confucian thought finds modern expression in Tate's regimented schedule.

These parallels reveal that **discipline is a timeless virtue**, reconceived here for the digital warrior.

4.7 Your 30-Day Discipline Gauntlet

To lock in the *Cobra Tate* standard, undertake this intensive discipline challenge:

1. **Week 1: Ritual Foundation**
    - Wake at the same early hour each day.
    - Identify and perform one keystone habit (e.g., morning workout, goal journaling).

2. **Week 2: Amplification**
    - Add a second habit via habit stacking (e.g., review finances post-lunch).
    - Implement the "never miss twice" rule for any lapse.

3. **Week 3: Environmental Mastery**
    - Audit your surroundings: eliminate one major distraction (e.g., social media, junk food).
    - Rearrange your workspace for focus—clear desk, only essential tools.

4. **Week 4: Measurement & Iteration**
    - Track every habit and metric in a visible dashboard.
    - At week's end, analyze successes and failures; refine your rituals for the next cycle.

This gauntlet will forge your capacity to **transform intention into action**, embedding discipline so deeply it becomes as automatic as breathing.

4.8 The Essence of Unbreakable Momentum

Discipline, once habituated, yields a force far greater than fleeting motivation. Andrew's final insight is this:

> "Discipline is the compound interest of personal excellence. Once you pay the price day after day, your return on investment multiplies beyond imagination."

In *Cobra Tate*, discipline is not an endpoint but a perpetual ascent. As you complete this chapter's gauntlet, you will possess the foundational architecture upon which all future victories—financial, physical, intellectual, and spiritual—are built.

Prepare now to channel this unbreakable discipline into your next transformative endeavor: the obsession for greatness awaits in Chapter 5.

"To be good you'll need motivation, but greatness requires obsession."
— **Tristan Tate**

Chapter 5: Motivation Is Not Enough — The Obsession for Greatness

In the grand theater of achievement, **motivation** is the flash of lightning that illuminates your path—but **obsession** is the thunder that shakes the earth beneath your feet. Andrew Tate insists that while motivation can spark action, only obsession sustains the indomitable drive required to ascend to the summit of any discipline. This chapter explores how to cultivate a compelling, all-consuming obsession, the rituals that anchor it, and the safeguards that ensure it fuels success rather than collapse.

5.1 The Motivation Myth

Most self-help doctrines trumpet motivation as the Elixir of Action, yet Andrew observes that:

- **Motivation is fleeting.** It waxes and wanes with mood, energy, and external circumstances.

- **Motivation demands justification.** You need an emotional hook—an inspiring quote, a promise of reward—to get moving.

- **Motivation invites complacency.** Once a short-lived surge passes, many revert to inertia.

Contrast this with **obsession**, which:

1. **Anchors to Identity:** It becomes a nonnegotiable part of who you are, not just what you do.

2. **Operates Independently of Mood:** When motivation ebbs, obsession pushes you forward anyway.

3. **Demands Sacrifice:** It compels you to prioritize your mission above comfort, entertainment, and even relationships.

Andrew's mantra is clear: *"If you rely on how you feel, you will fail. Let your obsession become your feeling."*

5.2 Obsession Defined: The Relentless Pursuit

Obsession, in Andrew's framework, is **the unstoppable compulsion** to close the gap between your current reality and your vision of excellence. Its defining characteristics include:

- **Singular Focus:** Your mind orbits your goal exclusively—other concerns become background noise.
- **Unyielding Routine:** You design your life around your mission, with every habit reinforcing the obsession.
- **Sacred Sacrifices:** You willingly forgo short-term pleasures—parties, idle scrolling, comfort food—to protect your pursuit.
- **Tunnel Vision:** You filter information, people, and opportunities through the lens of your obsession, discarding what doesn't serve it.

Obsession is not mere passion; it is **passion on steroids**—an all-in commitment that recognizes no Plan B.

5.3 Igniting Obsession: Rituals and Mindset Hacks

To cultivate obsession, Andrew prescribes a series of **ritualized ignitions**, each designed to bind you ever tighter to your mission:

5.3.1 The Daily "Vision Burn"

- **Morning Immersion (5 minutes):** Review a visual board or written manifesto describing your ultimate goal in vivid detail—as if already achieved.

- **Emotional Amplification:** Trigger the emotional centers of your brain—feel the thrill of victory, the respect of peers, the freedom of mastery.

5.3.2 The Micro-Goal Cascade

- **Break Down the Mountain:** Divide your grand vision into 90-day "summits," then into weekly "cliffs," and daily "steps."

- **Immediate Wins:** Begin each day by accomplishing the smallest step—this activates dopamine and cements your obsession habit.

5.3.3 Environment as Incubator

- **360° Reminders:** Surround yourself with cues—posters, notes, apps—that constantly remind you of your obsession.

- **Selective Exposure:** Unfollow social media accounts, avoid venues, and distance from people that dilute your focus.

5.3.4 Accountability Intensification

- **Public Contracts:** Post your daily or weekly targets on a public forum or tell a group of peers who will demand proof.

- **Obsession Partner:** Find one person equally obsessed with their goal; share progress calls daily to maintain mutual pressure.

These rituals transform obsession from an abstract desire into a **tangible, neurally embedded drive** that governs every waking moment.

5.4 Case Studies: Lives Transformed by Obsession

5.4.1 The Athlete Who Became Undefeated

A young boxer, inspired by Andrew's stories, adopted a 24/7 fight-camp mentality:

- **Visualizing Victory:** Spent 10 minutes before every sparring session visualizing the knockout blow.
- **Skill Saturation:** Reviewed fight footage overnight on a loop, imprinting tactics into his subconscious.
- **Lifestyle Alignment:** Ate, slept, and socialized strictly around his training schedule—no exceptions.

Result: He went from a 6–3 amateur record to a flawless 18–0 professional streak within two years, never showing hesitation or doubt in the ring.

5.4.2 The Entrepreneur Who Built a 7-Figure Amazon Empire

A former corporate drone dared to chase e-commerce glory:

- **Midnight Market Research:** An obsession so acute that he compiled product data past midnight, scrubbing Amazon and Alibaba for niches.
- **Algorithm Mastery:** Reverse-engineered Amazon's ranking system—running 50 split tests per week until he cracked the "buy box."
- **Automated Obsession:** Wrote scripts to monitor listing performance every hour, alerting him instantly to shifts, ensuring continuous optimization.

Outcome: In eighteen months, his private-label products generated over $2 million in revenue, and he sold the business for a significant multiple—**a direct payoff for obsessive mastery of details others ignored**.

5.4.3 The Artist Who Achieved Viral Mastery

A self-taught digital painter committed to breaking through obscurity:

- **100-Day Creation Challenge:** Posted one complete digital artwork daily, regardless of inspiration or feedback.
- **Community Love-Bombing:** Engaged obsessively with fellow artists and potential patrons—commenting, critiquing, and collaborating online.
- **Iterative Refinement:** After every post, solicited brutal feedback, then reworked the next piece to address every critique.

Result: One of her pieces exploded on social media, leading to gallery invitations, commission requests, and a rapidly growing subscriber base—**obsession turned a hidden talent into a public phenomenon.**

5.5 Safeguarding Your Obsession: Avoiding the Abyss

An obsession unchecked can devolve into **burnout** or **self-destructive tunnel vision**. Andrew warns of two fatal extremes:

1. **Workaholic Collapse:** Obsession without rest leads to exhaustion, injury, and mental breakdown.
2. **Social Isolation:** Cutting all personal connections can hollow you, removing emotional support structures.

To avoid these traps, implement the **Obsession Safety Net**:

- **Scheduled Recovery:** Block at least one 24-hour period per week—no work, no planning—dedicated to rest and joy.
- **Cross-Training:** Pursue a secondary, lower-pressure passion (music, hiking, reading) to replenish creativity and prevent single-minded fatigue.
- **Accountability Checks:** Weekly check-ins with a mentor or partner to ensure your obsession remains healthy and sustainable.

An obsession that eschews balance can consume you; a disciplined obsession anchored with recovery ensures **relentless longevity**.

5.6 Philosophical Underpinnings: Will to Power and Flow State

Andrew's obsession ethos echoes two profound concepts:

- **Nietzsche's Will to Power:** The drive to assert and enhance one's life-force—translated here as the urge to conquer every challenge and expand personal sovereignty.

- **Csikszentmihalyi's Flow:** The mental state of complete immersion where skill and challenge merge—obsession primes you for flow by ensuring each task is met with unwavering focus.

By integrating these philosophies into everyday practice, *Cobra Tate* obsession becomes both a **moral imperative** (to fulfill one's potential) and a **neurological supercharge** (to optimize brain function).

5.7 Your Obsession Plan: A 60-Day Deep Dive Protocol

To forge an obsession as potent as Andrew's, commit to this **60-Day Immersion**:

1. **Days 1–10: Define Your North Star**

    - Write a 1,000-word "obsession manifesto" detailing why your goal matters more than anything.

    - Share it publicly as a contract you cannot back away from.

2. **Days 11–30: Ritualization Phase**

    - Implement the Daily Vision Burn and Micro-Goal Cascade each morning.

    - Layer on Environment Engineering: transform your workspace into a shrine to your mission.

3. **Days 31–45: Accountability Intensification**

    - Launch daily progress reports to your Obsession Partner and public forum.

    - Schedule biweekly "trial by fire" challenges—high-stress scenarios that test your focus (e.g., impromptu pitch sessions, live demos).

4. **Days 46–60: Sustain and Scale**

    - Introduce weekly "recovery rituals" (cold plunge + sauna, creative side project, social gathering).

    - Evaluate outcomes: what rituals fueled progress? Which caused friction? Refine accordingly.

This structured immersion ensures your obsession moves from sporadic zeal into **an indestructible lifestyle**.

5.8 Binding Obsession to Purpose: Aligning Passion with Vision

True obsession is not meaningless mania—it is **purpose-driven intensity**. Andrew teaches that:

- **Purpose Brings Precision:** Obsession without clarity becomes chaos; a well-defined purpose focuses your compulsion on the most impactful actions.
- **Vision Anchors Sacrifice:** When the why is crystal clear, forfeiting leisure or comfort feels like a rite of passage rather than punitive deprivation.
- **Legacy Elevates Obsession:** Tying your personal mission to a broader legacy (family, community, impact) infuses your pursuit with enduring meaning.

Take time to revisit your manifesto: ensure it reflects not only what you want, but whom you want to serve and how you wish to be remembered.

5.9 Chapter Summary and Forward Look

Obsessive pursuit is the alchemy that turns mortal ambition into extraordinary reality. By distinguishing obsession from fleeting motivation, ritualizing your drive, safeguarding against burnout, and anchoring your intensity in clear purpose, you wield obsession as both **compass and engine** on your journey to greatness.

In the next chapter, **self-reliance** beckons—where you learn to stand as your own savior, transforming your obsession-driven efforts into **autonomous empowerment**. Prepare to internalize the ultimate truth: no one is coming to save you—you must become your own hero.

> "If you're a procrastinator, have fun staying poor. It sounds harsh but the reality is no one is coming to save you."
> — **Tristan Tate**

Chapter 6: Self-Reliance — No One Is Coming to Save You

In the universe of *Cobra Tate*, **self-reliance** stands as the bedrock of empowerment. It is the unshakeable conviction that your destiny lies in your own hands, and that **relying on others or waiting for external rescue is the surest path to mediocrity**. This chapter plunges into Andrew Tate's uncompromising tenet of radical self-responsibility, detailing the mindsets, daily practices, and real-world strategies that transform dependency into sovereign agency.

6.1 The Principle of Radical Ownership

At the core of self-reliance is **ownership**—the deliberate choice to accept total responsibility for every outcome in your life. Andrew Tate frames it as the ultimate act of freedom:

1. **No Excuses, No Blame:** Every setback, every failure is a mirror reflecting a gap in your actions, decisions, or mindset.

2. **Internal Locus of Control:** Instead of attributing success to luck or external circumstances, you recognize that **your choices** are the primary levers of change.

3. **Empowered Agency:** By owning both victories and defeats, you reclaim the ability to iterate, improve, and direct your path.

No rescue squad, no savior figure, no unearned handout—self-reliance demands that **you become the source of your own solutions**.

6.2 Origins of Tate's Self-Reliance Ethos

Andrew and Tristan's childhood was marked by upheaval and limited resources. Their mother, a single parent, worked tirelessly to keep food on the table. In that environment, **waiting for help was a luxury they could not afford**:

- **First Hustles:** As teenagers, Andrew sold pirated DVDs and cobbled together odd jobs—dog walking, lawn mowing, car washing—to fund training and travel to competitions.

- **No Safety Net:** When injuries or financial shortfalls struck, there was no fallback. They either figured out a solution or went without.

- **Forging Independence:** These early scrapes instilled the belief that **resourcefulness trumps resources**—if you can solve a problem, resources will follow; if you wait for resources, problems will accumulate.

This crucible of necessity forged the Tate brothers into staunch advocates of taking control rather than seeking saviors.

6.3 Daily Self-Reliance Rituals

Andrew advocates embedding self-reliance into your routine through targeted habits:

6.3.1 Morning Autonomy Session

- **Solo Planning (10 min):** Before checking messages or social media, sit quietly with your journal and map out your day's priorities. No external inputs.

- **Resource Audit:** Identify the single most critical resource you need (time, energy, equipment, information) and plan how to secure or allocate it yourself.

6.3.2 Skills-First Approach

- **Weekly Skill Block (1 hour):** Dedicate time to learning or refining a high-income skill (coding, writing, negotiation, digital marketing) that directly increases your independence.

- **Project-Based Learning:** Instead of passive consumption, apply new skills immediately by launching a mini-project—e.g., publish a short article, build a simple website, offer a micro-service.

6.3.3 "No-Ask" Challenge

- **Daily "No Ask" Period (2 hours):** For a designated window each day, refuse to ask anyone for help or information. Force yourself to research, troubleshoot, and solve solo.

- **Debrief:** Log what questions you had and how you answered them—this builds confidence in your ability to find solutions.

6.3.4 Emergency Preparedness Drill

- **Monthly Simulation:** Identify a critical failure scenario in your life (e.g., loss of income source, sudden expense, technology breakdown) and create a step-by-step contingency plan that you can execute alone.

- **Toolkit Assembly:** Maintain a "self-reliance kit" (emergency fund, essential contacts, software licenses, skill guides) that you update monthly.

6.4 Tactical Mindset Shifts

Andrew's self-reliance doctrine relies on a series of mindset reframes that hardwire autonomy:

- **"I Am the CEO of My Life":** Treat your priorities as shareholders—decisions must maximize returns on time and effort, not appease emotional whims.

- **"Problems Are Opportunities in Disguise":** Every obstacle is a test of your resourcefulness; overcoming it upgrades your skillset and fortifies independence.

- **"Fallback Is for the Weak":** Removing safety nets—financial or emotional—forces you to develop capacity and avoid complacency.

By repeating these reframes daily, your brain rewrites its default scripts: dependency becomes uncomfortable, while self-reliance feels natural and invigorating.

6.5 Case Studies: Sovereign Success

6.5.1 The Freelancer Who Cut the Middlemen

A graphic designer tired of platform fees and client gatekeepers decided to go direct:

1. **Personal Brand Launch:** Built a simple portfolio website using self-taught web skills.
2. **Direct Outreach Campaign:** Sent cold emails to target clients, leveraging no-ask challenge techniques to research and pitch without external guidance.
3. **Value-First Proposals:** Offered a risk-sharing model—partial payment on delivery—to bypass negotiation hurdles.

Result: Within three months, she doubled her rates, eliminated platform commissions, and secured six-figure annual contracts—all by relying solely on her own initiative and skills.

6.5.2 The Investor Who Built a Passive Income Fortress

An office worker tired of paycheck dependence applied Tate's self-reliance principles to investing:

- **Education Commitment:** Spent evenings mastering dividend investing and rental property analysis through books, courses, and simulator tools—no financial advisor.
- **Pilot Investment:** Acquired a small duplex, managing tenants, maintenance, and taxes personally.
- **Reinvestment Cycle:** Channeled rental profits into additional properties, scaling his portfolio without external capital raises or syndication.

Outcome: After five years, he generated enough passive income to replace his salary, achieving true financial self-reliance by **becoming both landlord and asset manager**.

6.5.3 The Startup Founder Who Bypassed Venture Capital

A tech entrepreneur, disillusioned with equity dilution, pursued a bootstrapped path:

- **Minimum Viable Product (MVP):** Built a lean prototype himself using learned coding skills; refused to hire developers until revenue began.
- **Grassroots Marketing:** Leveraged guerrilla tactics—cold outreach, community forums, strategic giveaways—to acquire initial users without ad budgets.
- **Revenue Reinvestment:** Plowed early profits back into product improvements and customer support, scaling sustainably.

Result: With zero outside funding, he grew to profitability in 18 months, retaining complete ownership and control.

6.6 Deep Adversity: The Test of Absolute Autonomy

True self-reliance reveals itself in crisis. Andrew recalls a year when global sanctions and platform bans cut off all his primary income channels overnight:

- **Shock Response:** Instead of despair, he activated his contingency plan—pivoting to a new set of digital products hosted on independent platforms.
- **Network Leverage:** Tapped his global "wolf pack" (War Room members) for advice and technical assistance, then repaid help by providing marketing to their ventures in return—**a symbiotic self-reliance network**.
- **Outcome:** He not only recovered his income streams but expanded them, demonstrating that robust self-reliance entails building reciprocal alliances rather than dependence on any single system.

6.7 Philosophical Foundations: Existential Agency

Andrew's self-reliance ethos resonates with classic existential thought:

- **Sartre's Radical Freedom:** We are condemned to be free—solely responsible for everything we choose, good or bad—mirrored in Tate's belief that excuses are abdications of this freedom.
- **Nietzsche's Self-Creation:** "Become who you are" is realized through unflinching self-authorship—Tate's blueprint for forging identity through autonomous action.

By weaving these philosophies into his pragmatic guidance, Andrew elevates self-reliance from mere hustle tactic to a **moral imperative**: living authentically requires self-creation unmediated by external saviors.

6.8 Your Self-Reliance Protocol: The 45-Day Autonomy Forge

To internalize sovereign agency, undertake this **45-Day Autonomy Forge**:

1. **Days 1–7: Ownership Audit**

   - List every domain where you rely on others for basic function (e.g., food prep, transportation, technical tasks).
   - Identify which dependencies you can remove or mitigate in the next month.

2. **Days 8–21: Skill Sprint**

   - Pick one dependency and replace it with a self-taught skill: learn to cook staple meals, perform basic car maintenance, or set up your own digital workspace.
   - Demonstrate mastery by completing a real-world task unassisted each week.

3. **Days 22–35: Crisis Simulation**

   - Choose a worst-case scenario relevant to you (income loss, tech failure, health emergency).
   - Draft and test a step-by-step response plan, including resource checklists and decision trees. Document and refine.

4. **Days 36–45: Network of Equals**

   - Identify three peers committed to self-reliance. Establish a reciprocal "autonomy alliance" with weekly check-ins: share challenges, resources, and feedback.
   - Ensure that the alliance emphasizes **mutual empowerment**, not reliance on any single member.

Completing this forge will birth a self-reliant mindset that thrives in uncertainty—transforming you from passive reactor into proactive architect of your fate.

6.9 Chapter Summary and Forward Look

Self-reliance is the **cornerstone** upon which all other *Cobra Tate* virtues stand. By adopting radical ownership, embedding autonomy rituals, and building reciprocal networks of equals, you cut the lifelines of dependence and step into the arena as your own hero.

Up next, wealth and freedom await in Chapter 7—where you will learn to master your money mindset, convert your newfound agency into financial sovereignty, and claim the independence that comes with true prosperity.

Embrace this chapter's gauntlet. No one will rescue you, but now you hold the tools to rescue yourself—forever.

> "Being poor, weak, and broke is your fault. The only person who can make you rich and strong is you. Build yourself."
> — **Tristan Tate**

Chapter 7: Wealth and Freedom — Mastering Your Money Mindset

Money is more than a tool—it is the oxygen of autonomy, the fuel for freedom, and the ultimate metric of impact in the world of *Cobra Tate*. In Andrew Tate's philosophy, financial mastery is **not** an optional byproduct of success but its indispensable cornerstone. This chapter unfolds Andrew's comprehensive blueprint for acquiring, growing, and safeguarding wealth. You will learn the mindsets that dissolve poverty thinking, the daily disciplines that compound income, the strategic pivots that seize opportunity, and the philosophical foundations that elevate money from mere numbers to a pathway for sovereignty.

7.1 The Poverty Paradigm vs. The Abundance Paradigm

Many live shackled by the **poverty paradigm**, a mindset characterized by scarcity, fear, and defeatism:

- **Scarcity Bias:** Believing resources—jobs, clients, capital—are limited and fiercely contested.

- **Victim Mentality:** Attributing financial struggles to external factors: economy, education, background.
- **Short-Term Thinking:** Prioritizing immediate gratification over strategic investment.

Andrew Tate condemns these attitudes as **self-imposed prisons**. In their place, he champions the **abundance paradigm**:

1. **Resource Multiplicity:** There are infinite opportunities to create value—new markets, digital platforms, emergent technologies.

2. **Accountable Empowerment:** Your decisions—how you spend, save, and invest—determine your outcome more than outside conditions.

3. **Compound Vision:** True wealth compounds over time; small, consistent choices yield exponential returns.

Shifting from poverty to abundance is the first—and most crucial—step on your path to financial emancipation.

7.2 Andrew Tate's Origin Story: From Zero to Millions

Understanding Andrew's own transformation provides concrete proof that his money mindsets work when implemented:

- **Early Hustles:**
    - **Laptop Arbitrage:** In his early 20s, he bought and sold secondhand laptops, capitalizing on regional price disparities.
    - **Webcam Enterprise:** Pivoted during the rise of broadband; co-founded a webcam service that scaled rapidly, generating six-figure monthly profits within months due to minimal overhead and high demand.
- **Investment Pivots:**
    - **Casino Ventures:** Opened casinos in Romania, leveraging local partnerships and reinvesting early profits into marketing and expansion.

- ○ **Cryptocurrency Plays:** Entered Bitcoin and altcoins when most dismissed digital currencies—securing early gains that propelled his net worth into the multimillion-dollar range.

- **Digital Empire:**

  - ○ **Hustler's University (The Real World):** Leveraged his notoriety and teaching ability to build a subscription-based educational platform with over 200,000 members, generating recurring revenue streams.

  - ○ **Social Media Monetization:** Turned massive followings on TikTok, YouTube, and Twitter into direct sales funnels for courses, affiliate products, and high-ticket coaching.

Through each pivot, Andrew exemplified two core principles: **see value where others see noise**, and **move decisively when the reward outweighs the risk**.

7.3 The Four Pillars of the Tate Wealth Framework

Andrew Tate distills financial mastery into four interdependent pillars:

1. **Income Diversification**

   - ○ **Active Income Streams:** Salaries, freelancing, consulting—effort-linked earnings with scaling potential.
   - ○ **Semi-Passive Income Streams:** Courses, membership sites, digital products—created once, sold repeatedly.
   - ○ **Passive Income Streams:** Investments in real estate, dividend stocks, royalties—requiring upfront capital and strategic patience.

2. **High-Income Skill Acquisition**

   - ○ **Copywriting & Persuasion:** The art of crafting messages that compel action, whether sales pages or negotiation tactics.
   - ○ **Sales & Closing:** Developing the psychology and process to convert prospects into paying clients.

- **Digital Marketing:** Mastering paid ads, funnel optimization, and analytics to scale ventures with precision.

3. **Strategic Risk Management**
    - **Calculated Leverage:** Using borrowed capital or partnerships when the upside justifies the potential downsides.
    - **Safeguarded Reserves:** Maintaining an emergency fund equal to six months of expenses to weather downturns without panic.
    - **Tax & Legal Optimization:** Employing corporations, trusts, and offshore vehicles (where lawful) to protect and multiply net assets.

4. **Compound Growth Mindset**
    - **Long-Term Orientation:** Prioritizing investments that may underperform short term but dominate over decades.
    - **Reinvestment Discipline:** Routinely channeling a percentage of profits back into your highest-return assets.
    - **Skill-and-Asset Synergy:** Aligning personal development with portfolio expansion—for example, investing in coaching to improve your own earning ability.

Together, these pillars form a **self-perpetuating engine**: skills generate income, income funds investments, investments bankroll new ventures, and continuous learning multiplies your capacity to profit.

7.4 Daily Wealth-Building Rituals

To embody the Tate Wealth Framework, Andrew recommends embedding these rituals into your routine:

7.4.1 Morning Profit Pulse (5:00 AM – 6:00 AM)

- **Market Scan:** Spend 15 minutes reviewing core assets—stock portfolios, crypto positions, ad campaigns—to spot anomalies or opportunities before markets awaken.

- **Deal Spotlight:** Identify one high-potential opportunity each day (undervalued stock, emerging niche, B2B lead) and allocate initial research time.
- **Profit Affirmation:** Write down your net-worth goal for the year and the daily progress needed to reach it. Reviewing this cements financial clarity and motivation.

7.4.2 Tactical Work Blocks (Throughout the Day)

- **Revenue Sprint (60–90 min):** Laser-focus on tasks that directly generate or preserve income—closing sales calls, writing sales copy, negotiating contracts.
- **Diversification Deep Dive (30 min):** Rotate weekly between learning a new income stream (e.g., affiliate marketing one week, real-estate due diligence the next).
- **Investment Execution (30 min):** Based on your prior research, execute a small trade, transfer funds into a savings vehicle, or finalize a deal.

7.4.3 Evening Financial Reflection (8:00 PM – 8:30 PM)

- **P&L Review:** Log the day's earnings and expenses in a digital tracker for real-time net-worth monitoring.
- **Opportunity Log:** Note any new ideas, contacts, or market shifts worth revisiting. This creates a pipeline of future ventures.
- **Reinvestment Plan:** Allocate a set percentage (e.g., 20–30%) of net daily profits into your priority assets before leisure begins.

By ritualizing wealth tasks—rather than improvising—you automate **financial discipline** and ensure that income creation and growth are baked into your lifestyle.

7.5 Case Studies: Wealth in Motion

7.5.1 The Side Hustler Who Built a Six-Figure Consulting Business

An IT professional, frustrated by corporate caps on raises, adopted Andrew's abundance mindset:

- **Niche Identification:** Leveraged internal expertise to offer cybersecurity audits to small businesses—an underserved market.

- **Value-Based Pricing:** Charged premium rates by bundling audits with tailored remediation plans, reflecting confidence in delivering outcomes.

- **Partnership Engine:** Formed alliances with web developers who referred clients in exchange for joint commission splits.

Within a year, his side hustle eclipsed his full-time salary, granting him leverage to negotiate a more flexible work contract—and eventually to exit his job entirely.

7.5.2 The Digital Creator Who Monetized Passion into Passive Income

A fitness influencer harnessed Andrew's framework:

- **Knowledge Product Launch:** Wrote and self-published a 60-page eBook on high-intensity home workouts, priced at $19.

- **Automated Funnel:** Set up targeted Facebook and Google ads to drive traffic into an email capture sequence, converting cold leads into buyers at a 3% rate.

- **Recurring Revenue Upgrade:** Transitioned eBook buyers into a $49/month online coaching membership community.

Result: She scaled to four-figure daily revenues with minimal incremental effort—**demonstrating the power of semi-passive and passive streams** when orchestrated skillfully.

7.5.3 The Real-Estate Novice Who Achieved Location Independence

A traveler-couple, inspired by financial freedom, acquired a small duplex:

- **Bootstrapped Down Payment:** Sold unwanted belongings, maximized savings through Tate-inspired austerity, and secured an FHA loan.

- **Hands-On Management:** Handled tenant screening, maintenance, and rent collection personally for the first year, saving management fees.

- **Portfolio Expansion:** Reinvested rental cash flow into crowdfunding deals on reputable platforms, diversifying into commercial real estate.

Within three years, their real estate assets generated enough monthly income to underwrite full-time travel—**a living testament to wealth as a gateway to freedom**.

7.6 Overcoming Financial Pitfalls

Even the most disciplined wealth-builders face pitfalls. Andrew identifies common traps and countermoves:

1. **Lifestyle Inflation:** "As income rises, expenses balloon."
   - **Tate's Fix:** Cap discretionary spending increases to a fixed percentage of additional income; automate the rest into investments.

2. **Analysis Paralysis:** "Too much data, too little action."
   - **Tate's Fix:** Use 80/20 heuristics—focus on the 20% of assets or deals that generate 80% of returns, then execute swiftly.

3. **Over-Leverage Risks:** "Borrowing to the eyeballs can yield bankruptcy."
   - **Tate's Fix:** Limit total debt-to-asset ratio below 50%; always maintain liquidity to cover interest and principal for 12 months.

4. **Lack of Skill Diversification:** "Relying on one income stream is brittle."
   - **Tate's Fix:** Maintain at least three independent income pillars—active, semi-passive, and passive—to ensure stability.

By preemptively addressing these challenges, you ensure your wealth engine hums smoothly through market storms and personal disruptions.

7.7 Philosophical Foundations: Money as a Tool for Sovereignty

Andrew's relationship with money transcends mere accumulation; he views wealth as **the means to exert personal sovereignty**:

- **Stoic Alignment:** Marcus Aurelius counseled using external wealth wisely but not letting it dominate your character—Tate similarly warns against being a "money slave."
- **Existential Freedom:** Jean-Paul Sartre's notion of absolute freedom finds modern expression: money enables you to choose your path unfettered by circumstance.
- **Utilitarian Impact:** Drawing on John Stuart Mill, Tate asserts that "the greatest prosperities generate the greatest good" —with wealth comes the capacity to uplift communities, create jobs, and support loved ones.

This philosophical framing ensures that the pursuit of wealth in *Cobra Tate* is both **selfish** (for personal autonomy) and **selfless** (as a force for wider impact).

7.8 Your Wealth Acceleration Plan: A 90-Day Financial Sprint

To operationalize this chapter's teachings, undertake the **90-Day Wealth Acceleration Sprint**:

1. **Days 1–15: Mindset Mastery & Audit**

   - Complete a detailed net-worth audit—list all assets, liabilities, and cash flows.
   - Identify and journal every poverty-paradigm belief; craft abundance affirmations to replace them.

2. **Days 16–45: Income Expansion Block**

   - Launch or optimize one new income stream—pick from active, semi-passive, or passive categories.
   - Apply high-income skill learning: commit to 30 minutes daily of targeted skill acquisition relevant to that stream.

3. **Days 46–75: Diversification & Protection**

   - Allocate a minimum of 20% of net profits into at least two different asset classes (e.g., stocks, real estate, crypto).
   - Establish your emergency reserve—six months' worth of fixed expenses—stored in a liquid, low-volatility vehicle.

4. **Days 76–90: Optimization & Scaling**
    - Review all revenue and investment performance; reallocate 10% of underperforming capital into your top-performing assets.
    - Automate at least two financial tasks (e.g., scheduled transfers, recurring ad campaigns, profit reinvestment scripts) to eliminate decision fatigue.

Completing this sprint will ignite both **momentum** and **structure** in your wealth journey, propelling you far beyond the constraints of traditional financial timelines.

7.9 Chapter Summary and Forward Look

In the grand architecture of *Cobra Tate* philosophy, wealth is the **statue's pedestal**—it elevates every other life domain into new dimensions of possibility. By shifting to an abundance paradigm, mastering the four pillars of income, embedding wealth rituals, and fortifying your finances against common pitfalls, you transform money from a source of anxiety into a wellspring of freedom.

Next, Chapter 8 will grant you the keys to Andrew's flagship program—**Hustler's University**—revealing how he packages these principles into a community-driven engine of empowerment. Prepare to peer behind the curtain and learn how to teach, market, and scale your own mastery.

Forge ahead: financial sovereignty awaits no one; it is claimed by those bold enough to build it themselves.

> "It's very hard to become rich and successful. So if you can't learn how to self-motivate, then it's never gonna happen for you."
> — **Tristan Tate**

Chapter 8: Teaching the Hustle — Inside Hustler's University

Hustler's University (now reborn as **The Real World**) is not merely an online course—it is the living embodiment of the *Cobra Tate* doctrine, distilled into a communal forge designed to transform motivated individuals into self-sufficient wealth creators. In this chapter, we peel back the curtain on Andrew Tate's flagship platform: its genesis, architectural design, teaching methodologies, community dynamics, success blueprints, and the rigorous protocols that bind knowledge to action. You will see how Hustler's University scales the Tate philosophy into millions of pockets worldwide, why its model disrupts traditional education, and how you can leverage its principles—whether you enroll or build your own analogous system—to amplify both learning and earning.

8.1 The Origin and Evolution of Hustler's University

8.1.1 From Private Mentorship to Public Platform

- **Early Mentorship:** Andrew and Tristan initially offered one-on-one coaching to fighters and entrepreneurs, charging premium rates but reaching only dozens of clients.
- **Demand Outstrips Supply:** Word spread of their unfiltered, results-driven guidance; inboxes overflowed, and a scalable solution was required to democratize access.
- **Birth of the "University" (2020):** Leveraging a Discord server, they invited small cohorts of students to learn diverse skills—copywriting, crypto trading, e-commerce—directly from vetted "professors."

8.1.2 Rapid Growth and Rebranding

- **Viral Momentum:** Strategic use of TikTok and YouTube clips showcasing student success stories propelled enrollment from hundreds to tens of thousands in months.
- **Administrative Maturation:** The brothers recruited operational leads, built proprietary dashboards for progress tracking, and instituted a tiered "VIP" mentorship layer.
- **Transition to The Real World (2023):** A rebrand emphasizing actionable mastery over academia, with expanded curricula and a refocused mission: *"Equip every member to escape the Matrix."*

8.2 The Architectural Design: Learning as a Battlefield

8.2.1 Modular Skill "Faculties"

Hustler's University is divided into **faculties**, each led by a "professor" who demonstrates real-world success. Key faculties include:

Faculty	Core Focus	Delivery Mode
E-Commerce	Dropshipping, private-label brands	Live workshops + video modules
Copywriting	Sales pages, emails, ad creatives	Weekly critiques + templates
Crypto & Trading	Spot trading, futures, arbitrage	Daily market calls + playbooks
Freelancing	Upwork, Fiverr optimization	Portfolio reviews + case study
Investing	Dividend stocks, REITs, ETFs	Model portfolios + simulations
Social Media	Algorithm hacking, content calendars	Hot-seat coaching + analytics

Each faculty operates like a mini-academy, complete with lesson plans, resource libraries, and actionable assignments.

8.2.2 The "War Room" Framework

Beyond the faculties lies the **War Room**—an exclusive mastermind network open only to top performers. It functions as:

- **Strategic Command Center:** Biweekly live strategy sessions with Andrew, Tristan, and guest experts.
- **Accountability Pods:** 5–7 member subgroups that meet daily to share metrics, challenges, and breakthroughs.
- **Opportunity Exchange:** A private marketplace where members post joint-venture proposals, deal flow, and mentorship offers.

The War Room turns collective ambition into a multiplier: individual efforts feed into group intelligence, accelerating every member's trajectory.

8.3 Teaching Methodologies: From Theory to Combat-Ready Skill

8.3.1 "Learn—Apply—Master" Cycle

1. **Learn (30%)**

   - **Concise Modules:** Bite-sized video lessons (5–15 minutes) packed with frameworks and examples.
   - **Reading Lists:** Curated articles, book excerpts, and research papers to deepen theoretical grounding.

2. **Apply (50%)**

   - **Real-World Assignments:** Students launch live projects—ad campaigns with real budgets, test e-commerce stores, mock trading accounts with capital at risk.
   - **Hot-Seat Sessions:** Weekly live calls where students present progress, receive critique, and iterate immediately.

3. **Master (20%)**

   - **Peer Teaching:** Advanced students mentor newcomers, solidifying their own expertise.
   - **Performance Badges:** Digital credentials awarded for reaching key milestones—first sale, first profitable trade, first paid client.

8.3.2 Feedback Loops and Iterative Learning

- **Continuous Assessment:** Automated quizzes after each module ensure comprehension, with instant remediation prompts.
- **Mentor Office Hours:** Scheduled slots where students can book 15-minute one-on-one calls with faculty to troubleshoot roadblocks.
- **Data-Driven Iteration:** The platform tracks student engagement metrics—time spent, quiz scores, assignment completion—and uses A/B testing to optimize module order and content clarity.

8.4 Community Dynamics: Brotherhood, Competition, and Collaboration

8.4.1 The Culture of "Constructive Aggression"

- **Peer Challenges:** Regular "Shark Tank" style pitch nights where members compete to present business ideas; winners earn seed funding from alumni.
- **Leaderboards:** Public rankings for metrics like first-month revenues, quiz mastery, or daily engagement to stoke healthy competition.
- **Reward Systems:** Points redeemed for coaching sessions, exclusive workshops, or War Room access—fueling a gamified environment.

8.4.2 Mutual Accountability and Support

- **Accountability Partners:** Each student is paired with a partner for daily check-ins, reinforcing the habit of reporting progress and setbacks.
- **Emergency Channels:** Dedicated Discord threads for urgent problem-solving—technical errors, negotiating contracts, or crisis mindset coaching.
- **Alumni Network:** Graduates host monthly regional meetups and online reunions, fostering lifelong connections that extend beyond the digital campus.

8.5 Success Blueprints: Scaling Impact From Student to Teacher

8.5.1 Alumni-Led Faculties

High-performing graduates are invited to become **Associate Professors**:

- **Curriculum Development:** They co-create new modules reflecting emerging trends—NFTs, AI automation, cross-border e-commerce.

- **Peer Mentorship:** Lead small cohorts, sharpening their leadership skills while ensuring the platform's relevance.

- **Revenue Sharing:** Earn a share of tuition from students in their sub-faculty, creating an incentive to uphold quality and innovation.

8.5.2 Franchise Model: Beyond One University

Andrew envisions **"Hustler's University Licenses"**:

- **Local Editions:** Country-specific versions focusing on regional market nuances—e.g., dropshipping in Southeast Asia, real estate syndication in Europe.

- **Branded Partnerships:** Collaboration with established institutions to integrate Tate modules into business school curricula, expanding reach.

- **White-Label Programs:** Companies purchase a turnkey Hustler's framework to coach their own employees, infusing the hustle culture into corporate training.

8.6 Case Studies: Transformative Journeys

8.6.1 From Unemployed to Agency Owner

A recent graduate launched a digital marketing agency within 90 days:

- **Faculty Engagement:** Completed all copywriting modules and sales workshops.

- **War Room Pitch:** Secured a $5,000 paid pilot with a telecom client after a live online pitch judged by peers.

- **Scaling Tactics:** Hired two other HU alumni on profit-split terms; within six months, revenue exceeded $200,000.

8.6.2 The Crypto Trader Who Beat the Market

A student, starting with a $1,000 investment, achieved 30% monthly returns for six consecutive months:

- **Daily Market Calls:** Attended Tristan's live trading sessions at 6 AM to catch Asian market movements.

- **Signal Testing:** Backtested 20 different algorithmic trading strategies taught in course materials, refining them in simulated environments.

- **Risk Protocol:** Implemented Andrew's 1–3% capital-per-trade rule and stop-loss orders religiously, avoiding catastrophic drawdowns.

8.6.3 The E-Commerce Empire Built on a Shoestring

A fitness influencer turned HU member:

- **Niche Research Hack:** Used a custom spreadsheet tool shared by the E-Commerce faculty to identify "low-competition, high-demand" fitness accessories.

- **Supplier Negotiation Drill:** Applied copywriting and psychology lessons to negotiate exclusive deals with manufacturers in China.

- **Sales Funnel Automation:** Connected Shopify to email marketing and retargeting ads, all learned through HU's technical deep-dive labs.

Her store grew from zero to $50,000 monthly revenue in four months—proof that **the Hustler's method can accelerate even part-time entrepreneurs**.

8.7 Pitfalls and Corrections: Ensuring Quality and Integrity

8.7.1 Overpromising vs. Underperforming

- **Pitfall:** Inflated marketing "get rich quick" rhetoric leads to unrealistic expectations.

- **Tate's Correction:** Emphasize **"long game reality"**—most students require 3–6 months of dedicated work before achieving significant results.

8.7.2 Content Saturation and Outdated Modules

- **Pitfall:** Static curricula risk obsolescence in fast-moving fields.
- **Tate's Correction:** Mandatory quarterly content audits and faculty workshops to update case studies, revoke ineffective tactics, and integrate new tools.

8.7.3 Community Toxicity

- **Pitfall:** Fierce competition can foster negativity or elitism.
- **Tate's Correction:** Institute a **Code of Conduct** with zero tolerance for harassment; celebrate collaborative successes publicly; rotate leaderboard metrics to reward diverse forms of achievement (e.g., best mentor, most supportive peer).

8.8 Philosophical Foundations: Pedagogy of Action

Andrew's teaching philosophy synthesizes several educational and philosophical currents:

- **Pragmatic Constructivism:** Knowledge emerges through action and reflection—akin to John Dewey's experiential learning, but turbocharged with real-world stakes.
- **Socratic Provocation:** Faculty challenge assumptions via pointed questions rather than lectures—mirroring Socratic dialogues but with the urgency of business deadlines.
- **Nietzschean Self-Overcoming:** Students are encouraged to surpass their former limits in every cycle—championing Nietzsche's ideal of the Übermensch as self-made architects of destiny.

This **pedagogy of action** ensures that Hustler's University is not a repository of content, but a crucible of transformation.

8.9 Your Own "University in a Box": Building a Scalable Learning Ecosystem

Even if you never enroll, you can replicate the Hustler's blueprint in your own ventures:

1. **Identify Core Skills:** Choose 3–5 high-impact competencies you wish to teach.
2. **Develop Modular Content:** Create short, actionable video lessons with accompanying worksheets.
3. **Implement Feedback Loops:** Use quizzes, hot-seat reviews, and peer mentoring to cement learning.
4. **Cultivate Community:** Launch a Slack or Discord channel with accountability pods and public leaderboards.
5. **Scale Faculty:** Recruit top performers as guest mentors, offering revenue share to maintain quality.

By packaging knowledge into an ecosystem of **teach—apply—master**, you harness the same forces that propelled Hustler's University to global prominence.

8.10 Chapter Summary and Forward Look

Hustler's University stands as a testament to the scalability of the *Cobra Tate* philosophy: transforming authoritarian mentorship into a distributed network of self-driven learners, fueled by competition, collaboration, and uncompromising action. You have seen how its architecture, methodologies, and community dynamics converge to accelerate mindsets and bank accounts alike.

In the next chapter, we turn inward once more, focusing on **Strength and Fitness**—the physical pillar of Tate's triumvirate of mind, money, and muscle. Prepare to explore how a warrior's physique undergirds both confidence and competence in every arena of life.

Forge your own path: whether as student or architect of a new learning empire, you now hold the blueprint to teach the hustle—and to teach yourself to hustle even harder.

> "You can change how rich you are. You can change how fit you are. You can change how smart you are. Almost everything in your life is within your control."
> — **Tristan Tate**

Chapter 9: Strength and Fitness — The Warrior's Physique

In *Cobra Tate* philosophy, the body is both temple and weapon. Physical strength fuels mental resilience, sharpens focus, and projects confidence that commands respect—internally and externally. This chapter unveils Andrew Tate's exhaustive system for forging a warrior's physique: from foundational principles and personal origin stories to daily training protocols, nutritional engineering, recovery science, real-world transformations, common pitfalls, and the deeper philosophical underpinnings uniting mind and muscle. By the end, you will possess a bespoke, 12-week blueprint to sculpt strength, endurance, and vitality that fortifies every aspect of your life.

9.1 The Imperative of Physical Mastery

Andrew's creed: **"A weak body begets a weak mind."** His teachings rest on three immutable truths:

1. **Fitness as a Force Multiplier:** Physical capability amplifies confidence, decision-making under stress, and the capacity to endure hardship.

2. **Discipline Through Repetition:** Consistent training inculcates habits of excellence—each rep a commitment to your broader mission.

3. **Embodied Credibility:** Strength commands respect; a well-developed physique signals that you live by your own standards, not idle words.

He often reminds followers that modern comforts have bred physical atrophy; reclaiming your primal strength is a reclamation of **sovereignty over your own vessel**.

9.2 Andrew Tate's Origin Story: From Kickboxing Champion to Fitness Evangelist

9.2.1 The Early Combat Years

- **First Steps:** Andrew began martial arts at age ten—karate, judo, then kickboxing—learning to wield his body as a strategic instrument.
- **Champion's Routine:** At 18, his training schedule peaked at 2–3 sessions daily:
    - **Morning:** Roadwork—10 km runs, sprint intervals on hills for explosive power.
    - **Midday:** Technical drills—pad work, clinch wrestling, sparring rounds.
    - **Evening:** Strength & conditioning—Olympic lifts, plyometrics, core fortification.

9.2.2 Transition to Lifestyle Fitness

After stepping away from pro fighting, Andrew maintained his regimen, adapting to an entrepreneur's schedule:

- **Efficiency Upgrades:** Condensed workouts into 45-minute sessions combining resistance training and metabolic conditioning—maximizing results under time constraints.
- **Functional Focus:** Integrated bodyweight movements (muscle-ups, pistols, handstand push-ups) to preserve agility, coordination, and proportional strength.

This evolution demonstrates that **elite fitness transcends pure sport**, becoming a lifelong practice of self-mastery.

9.3 The Four Foundational Pillars of the Tate Fitness System

Andrew Tate's fitness philosophy coalesces into four interdependent pillars:

1. **Progressive Resistance Training**
    - **Compound Movements:** Squat, deadlift, bench press, and overhead press form the core, stimulating systemic growth.
    - **Periodization:** Four-week blocks alternating between hypertrophy (8–12 reps) and strength (3–5 reps) phases.

2. **Explosive Athletic Conditioning**

    - **Plyometrics:** Box jumps, kettlebell swings, medicine-ball slams for fast-twitch recruitment.
    - **Sprinting Protocols:** Hill sprints and shuttle runs to develop anaerobic power.

3. **Mobility and Stability**

    - **Dynamic Flexibility:** Daily dynamic warm-ups (leg swings, shoulder circles) to maintain joint range.
    - **Stability Drills:** Single-leg Romanian deadlifts and anti-rotation presses to prevent injury and enhance balance.

4. **Nutrition as Fuel and Sculpture**

    - **Macronutrient Precision:** Protein 1.2–1.5 g per pound of lean weight; carbs timed around workouts; healthy fats for hormonal health.
    - **Cycling Strategies:** Periodic carb refeeding days and controlled caloric deficits to optimize body composition while preserving performance.

These pillars interact: strength work enhances sprint power, mobility sustains lift quality, and nutrition supplies the raw materials for adaptation.

9.4 Daily Training and Nutrition Protocol

To actualize the Tate Fitness System, adhere to the following daily regimen:

9.4.1 Morning Activation (6:00 AM – 7:00 AM)

- **Dynamic Warm-Up (6:00 – 6:10):** Leg swings, inchworms, world's greatest stretch.
- **Sprint or Plyo Session (6:10 – 6:30):**
    - Hills: 8 × 30-meter sprints with 90-second rest.
    - OR Box Jump Ladder: 5–8–10 reps increasing box height each set.

- **Mobility Circuit (6:30 – 7:00):** Foam rolling (glutes, quads, lats), hip-openers, thoracic extensions against a foam roller.

9.4.2 Midday Strength Block (12:00 PM – 1:00 PM)

- **Warm-Up Sets:** Two light sets of the day's compound lift.
- **Main Lift (3–5 sets):**
    - Strength phase: 3–5 reps at RPE 8–9.
    - Hypertrophy phase: 8–12 reps at RPE 7–8.
- **Accessory Circuits (15 min):**
    - Push–Pull Supersets: Incline dumbbell press + bent-over row (4 × 10 each).
    - Core Tri-Set: Hanging leg raises, Pallof press, back extensions (3 × 12 each).

9.4.3 Evening Stability and Recovery (7:00 PM – 8:00 PM)

- **Yoga-Style Flow (20 min):** Sun salutations, warrior sequences to enhance flexibility and calm the nervous system.
- **Stability Drills (20 min):** Single-leg squats, bird-dog holds, TRX suspension rows focusing on control and proprioception.
- **Cold Therapy (10 min):** Ice bath or cold shower to reduce inflammation and accelerate muscle repair.
- **Active Recovery (10 min):** Light walking or cycling to promote circulation.

9.4.4 Nutrition Timeline

- **Pre-Workout (5:30 AM):** 20g hydrolyzed whey, 10g BCAAs, small banana.
- **Post-Workout (7:15 AM):** 40g whey, 50g dextrose, creatine monohydrate.
- **Lunch (1:00 PM):** 8 oz grilled chicken, 1 cup quinoa, mixed greens, olive oil dressing.

- **Snack (4:00 PM):** Greek yogurt with berries and walnuts.
- **Dinner (8:30 PM):** 8 oz salmon or lean beef, roasted vegetables, sweet potato.
- **Evening Shake (10:00 PM):** Casein protein to sustain overnight recovery.

Hydration: Minimum 1 gallon water daily, electrolytes added to one liter to maintain performance and cognitive clarity.

9.5 Periodized 12-Week Strength Cycle

To ensure continual progress and avoid plateaus, follow this structured cycle:

Weeks	Focus	Weekly Layout
1–4	Hypertrophy	4 days lifting (8–12 reps), 2 days conditioning, 1 active rest
5–8	Strength	3 days heavy lifts (3–5 reps), 2 days plyos, 2 active rest
9–10	Power & Speed	Olympic lift derivatives + sprint work, 2 days hypertrophy circuits
11–12	Peak & Deload	Week 11: max testing for squat/bench/deadlift; Week 12: 60% volume for recovery

Track weekly metrics—weights lifted, sprint times, body measurements—to calibrate load and ensure linear adaptation.

9.6 Case Studies: Warrior Transformations

9.6.1 The Deskbound Executive Turned Spartan

A 38-year-old executive, sedentary for years, adopted Tate's 12-week cycle:

- **Initial Assessment:** BMI 29, zero morning energy.

- **Week 1–4:** Lost 12 pounds, gained 8 lbs lean mass, improved squat from 135 to 185 lbs.

- **Week 5–8:** Squat 225 lbs×5, bench 185 lbs×5; shaved 1 second off 40-yard sprint.

- **Week 9–12:** Completed 100 consecutive burpees in 8 minutes, 120-lb power clean for 3 reps.

Result: Transitioned from breathless meeting attendee to morning Spartan, inspiring corporate wellness programs and hosting weekly "office Spartans" group workouts.

9.6.2 The Martial Artist Who Regained Peak Performance

A former amateur MMA fighter, sidelined by injuries, rebuilt himself using Tate's fusion of mobility and strength:

- **Injury Rehab Integration:** Mobility drills to restore range of motion after shoulder surgery.

- **Strength Redirection:** Replaced bench press with landmine presses to respect joint health while building pressing power.

- **Performance Metrics:** Recorded a 20% increase in takedown defense success rate and returned to competition at a performance level matching his pre-injury peak.

His comeback victory was lauded as "phenomenal" by coaches—demonstrating how Andrew's approach balances **vigor and longevity**.

9.7 Overcoming Common Pitfalls

Even the most disciplined can stumble. Andrew identifies obstacles and prescriptions:

1. **Stagnation Plateau:** When progress stalls, volume jumps cause overtraining.
    - **Fix:** Implement immediate 10% volume reduction and reintroduce progressive overload via micro-increments (2.5–5 lbs).

2. **Injury Risk:** Ego lifts or skipping warm-ups leads to setbacks.

   - **Fix:** Prioritize joint warm-ups, mobility maintenance days, and strict form cues—even dialing back loads if necessary.

3. **Nutrition Slippage:** Busy schedules lead to inconsistent meal timing.

   - **Fix:** Meal-prep on Sundays—freeze portions—and schedule eating reminders on your phone; treat them as non-negotiable meetings.

4. **Motivation Crashes:** Initial enthusiasm wanes after weeks of hard work.

   - **Fix:** Introduce novelty—new exercises, seasonal outdoor workouts, fitness challenges with peers—to rekindle engagement.

By anticipating and engineering safeguards, your training remains **resilient** against life's unpredictability.

9.8 Philosophical Foundations: The Body–Mind Synergy

Andrew's fitness ideology resonates with timeless doctrines:

- **Aristotelian Eudaimonia:** The flourishing life is lived through virtuous action—here, virtuous care for the body yields happiness and capability.

- **Yamamoto Tsunetomo's Bushido:** The samurai code emphasizes physical discipline as moral training; Tate's regimen serves a similar **ethical function**, instilling courage and honor.

- **Mindfulness in Motion:** Borrowing from Zen, Tate's emphasis on presence during training transforms each rep into a meditative act, sharpening focus for all life domains.

Thus, your workouts become **philosophical practice**, bridging the gap between flesh and spirit.

9.9 Your 12-Week Warrior's Blueprint

To actualize a transformation worthy of *Cobra Tate*, undertake this **comprehensive 12-week guide**:

1. **Weeks 1–4: Foundation & Form**
   - Master movement patterns (squat, hinge, push, pull).
   - Establish baseline nutrition; track macros and hydration religiously.
   - Perform mobility routine daily; progress to stability drills.

2. **Weeks 5–8: Strength & Explosiveness**
   - Shift to low-rep heavy lifts; integrate plyometrics post-strength session.
   - Increase sprint volume; add resisted sprints (sled or parachute) for power.
   - Refine nutrition for strength—slight caloric surplus with high protein.

3. **Weeks 9–10: Power & Speed Emphasis**
   - Incorporate Olympic lift variations (hang cleans, push jerks) for neuromuscular recruitment.
   - Reduce volume midweek for fresher speed sessions; test 10-meter and 40-yard sprint PRs.
   - Introduce strategic carb cycling around intense workouts.

4. **Weeks 11–12: Peak & Recovery**
   - Perform 1RM tests for squat, bench, deadlift; record results.
   - Deload week: 60% volume, enhanced focus on mobility, cold therapy, and active rest.
   - Plan next cycle based on data—adjust loads, sprint targets, and nutrition strategy.

Document every session, measurement, and subjective energy rating. By chapter's end, you'll possess **quantifiable proof** of your metamorphosis and the metrics to guide future mastery.

9.10 Chapter Summary and Forward Look

Physical strength is the **tangible expression** of every other Tate virtue—fearlessness, resilience, discipline, obsession, self-reliance, and wealth. A warrior's physique is not an end in itself, but the platform upon which all victories—personal, professional, philosophical—stand unshakable.

Next, Chapter 10 delves into Andrew Tate's most debated domain: **Masculinity**. You will explore how to harness your newfound strength and freedom into purposeful manhood, adopt a commanding presence, and lead with both power and integrity in a world hungry for authentic leadership.

Prepare your body, mind, and spirit: the true journey of *Cobra Tate* marches on.

> "You have to understand that life is war. It's a war for the female you want. It's a war for the car you want. It's a war for the money you want. Masculine life is war."
> — Tristan Tate

Chapter 10: Masculinity — Embracing Manhood with Purpose

Masculinity, in the *Cobra Tate* paradigm, is not a fossilized relic of bygone eras but a living, breathing force: **the driver of purpose, protector of values, and architect of legacy**. In this exhaustive chapter, we unpack Andrew Tate's uncompromising vision of modern manhood—its origins, core virtues, daily disciplines, strategic frameworks, real-world exemplars, common missteps, philosophical underpinnings, and a 60-day "Warrior of Purpose" protocol. By embracing purposeful masculinity, you will learn to wield your strength, integrity, and leadership in every arena of life.

10.1 The Essence of Purposeful Masculinity

Andrew Tate asserts that **manhood is defined by responsibility, competition, and service**. At its heart lie three pillars:

1. **Duty to Provide and Protect**

- **Provision:** Securing resources—financial, emotional, strategic—for yourself and those you care for.
- **Protection:** Cultivating physical strength, mental resilience, and moral courage to stand as a bulwark against threats.

2. **Competitive Excellence**
    - **Self-Competition:** Measuring yourself against your past performance, not others' mediocrity.
    - **Respect Through Merit:** Earning esteem by demonstrating capability in your chosen field, whether business, art, or community leadership.

3. **Purpose-Driven Leadership**
    - **Vision Casting:** Defining a clear mission—professional, familial, or societal—and inspiring others to follow.
    - **Integrity in Action:** Aligning words and deeds so that trust becomes your most potent currency.

Masculinity, then, is **the dynamic interplay** between strength and service, ambition and honor, self-mastery and collective uplift.

10.2 Origins of Tate's Masculine Doctrine

10.2.1 Lessons from the Ring

- **Combat as Metaphor:** Every match taught Andrew that dominance requires both power and strategy. He translated ring tactics—timing, distance control, feints—into life lessons on negotiation, conflict resolution, and leadership.

- **Resilience Under Fire:** Repeated knockdowns forged the belief that a true man stands again, not because he must, but because he *will*.

10.2.2 Family and Fraternity

- **Paternal Legacy:** Their father, Emory Tate, exemplified intellectual ferocity. Andrew learned that mental aggression must be matched by ethical restraint—a warrior's discipline guided by conscience.

- **Brotherly Brotherhood:** With Tristan as ally, Andrew internalized loyalty and accountability: two pillars that transform individual strength into a collective force.

10.3 The Five Fundamental Virtues of Modern Manhood

Andrew condenses masculinity into five interlocking virtues:

1. **Courage**

    - **Moral Courage:** Upholding truth even when unpopular.

    - **Physical Courage:** Willingness to face danger to protect values and loved ones.

2. **Discipline**

    - As in Chapter 4, the bedrock that transforms intention into habit, ensuring that every day you forge yourself into a more capable man.

3. **Competence**

    - Expertise in chosen fields—financial acumen, physical prowess, strategic thinking—so that others rely on your judgment.

4. **Confidence**

    - Radiant self-assurance born from preparation and past victories; a magnet for respect and opportunities.

5. **Compassion**

    - Acknowledging that true strength is validated through the upliftment of others—family, community, protégés—balancing warrior's might with gentleman's grace.

These virtues form an **ethical code**: a blueprint for living with purpose, power, and principle.

10.4 Daily Rituals of Purposeful Manhood

To embody these virtues, Andrew prescribes a regimented daily slate that channels masculine energy constructively:

10.4.1 Dawn of Duty (5:00 AM – 6:00 AM)

- **Mindful Meditation (5 min):** Center on your mission statement—why you rise, whom you serve, what legacy you build.
- **Gratitude & Charge (5 min):** Journal three things you're grateful for and three battles you will conquer today.
- **Warrior's Workout (50 min):** Integrate strength, conditioning, and martial drills—each set symbolizing a personal conquest.

10.4.2 Morning Council (8:00 AM – 9:00 AM)

- **Strategic Briefing:** Review top three priorities aligned with your vision—family commitments, business milestones, personal development.
- **Accountability Rally:** Touch base with your "warrior circle" via group chat—report yesterday's wins and today's objectives.

10.4.3 Midday Mastery (12:00 PM – 1:00 PM)

- **Skill Sharpening:** One focused hour on a high-value skill—public speaking, financial modeling, leadership frameworks.
- **Power Networking:** Initiate or respond to two outreach messages—mentors, peers, protégés—to strengthen your influence web.

10.4.4 Evening Reflection & Brotherhood (7:00 PM – 8:00 PM)

- **Battle Report:** Document today's victories and defeats—what you learned, how you'll adapt.
- **Fraternal Feast:** Share a meal with close allies or family, exchanging candid reflections and mutual support.

This **rhythmic structure** binds your daily actions to your overarching masculine purpose.

10.5 Strategic Masculinity Frameworks

Andrew teaches specialized frameworks to operationalize masculine leadership:

10.5.1 The "Five Battlegrounds" Model

Map your life into five arenas—Health, Wealth, Relationships, Influence, and Legacy. For each:

1. **Assess Current Strength:** Rate yourself 1–10.
2. **Define Next Objective:** Clear, measurable, and aligned with your vision.
3. **Allocate Resources:** Time, energy, capital, mentorship.
4. **Execute Tactics:** Specific drills, learning modules, outreach campaigns.
5. **Review & Iterate:** Weekly scorecards and adjustment plans.

10.5.2 The "Alpha Resonance" Method

Cultivate an "alpha presence" that naturally commands respect:

- **Vocal Intonation:** Speak slowly, with measured volume and cadence—projecting calm authority.
- **Postural Dominance:** Maintain strong posture—open chest, squared shoulders, steady gaze.
- **Status Signaling:** Subtle displays of competence—phygital props like a well-tailored suit, disciplined physique, punctuality.

This method teaches that **masculine energy communicates as much through presence as through words**.

10.6 Case Studies: Exemplars of Purposeful Manhood

10.6.1 The CEO Who Led Through Crisis

A startup founder faced collapse during an industry downturn. He:

- **Declared "Battle Stations"**—all-hands daily standups to triage challenges.
- **Redirected Resources**—scaled back non-essential projects and doubled down on profitable pivot opportunities.
- **Communicated Transparently**—honest town-hall meetings bolstered team trust.

Outcome: The company returned to growth within six months, with employee morale higher than ever—**a testament to masculine leadership under fire.**

10.6.2 The Father Who Reclaimed His Role

A high-earning father felt disconnected from his children. Inspired by Andrew:

- **Structured Quality Time:** Instituted "father–child missions"—hiking, workshop building, financial literacy sessions.
- **Embodied Consistency:** Showed up early for school events and bedtime rituals, demonstrating that **masculinity is measured in reliability, not bravado.**

Relationships deepened; his kids showed improved academic and social confidence—**proof that purposeful masculinity uplifts the next generation.**

10.6.3 The Community Leader Who Mobilized Change

A local entrepreneur saw his neighborhood plagued by youth idleness. He:

- **Launched "Warrior Saturdays":** Free martial-arts and fitness classes for at-risk youth.
- **Mentorship Pods:** Paired young participants with veterans in trades, facilitating apprenticeships.
- **Resource Partnerships:** Collaborated with local businesses to sponsor equipment and job placements.

Impact: Juvenile delinquency rates dropped, employment among graduates rose, and the community gained renewed pride—**a demonstration of masculinity as collective service.**

10.7 Pitfalls and Corrections: Avoiding Toxic Extremes

Masculine agency can tip into toxicity without guardrails. Andrew warns against:

1. **Hyper-Aggression:** Unchecked dominance devolves into bullying.

   - **Correction:** Temper courage with compassion—question: "Does this action uplift or harm?"

2. **Emotional Stoicism:** Suppressing vulnerability leads to isolation and poor mental health.

   - **Correction:** Practice "structured vulnerability"—sharing challenges with trusted allies.

3. **Identity Rigidity:** Defining manhood too narrowly excludes growth paths.

   - **Correction:** Embrace adaptability—recognize that modern masculinity can include nurturer, innovator, and protector roles.

4. **Overextension:** Trying to conquer every battleground at once leads to burnout.

   - **Correction:** Prioritize one or two arenas at a time—apply the 80/20 rule to your masculine focus.

By integrating these corrective measures, your masculine purpose remains **healthy, holistic, and enduring**.

10.8 Philosophical Underpinnings: Warrior Ethics and Virtue

Andrew's masculine vision draws upon enduring philosophical traditions:

- **Aristotelian Virtue Ethics:** The "golden mean" of courage—neither rashness nor cowardice but the balanced excellence that leads to eudaimonia.

- **Confucian Duty:** The concept of *li*—ritual propriety—mirrored in disciplined daily rites and family responsibilities.

- **Nietzschean Overman:** The call to self-overcome and craft one's own values, forging identity beyond societal scripts.

These foundations root *Cobra Tate* masculinity in **timeless wisdom**, reimagined for the 21st-century warrior.

10.9 Your 60-Day "Warrior of Purpose" Protocol

To seize your masculine potential, embark on this **60-day immersion**:

1. **Days 1–10: Pillar Alignment**

    - Articulate your mission in each battleground.
    - Draft a 5-year masculine vision: provider, protector, leader, legacy.

2. **Days 11–30: Ritual Implementation**

    - Solidify daily rituals (Section 10.4).
    - Launch "Morning Council" and "Evening Brotherhood" gatherings.

3. **Days 31–45: Strategic Execution**

    - Execute the Five Battlegrounds Model: set metrics and hit weekly milestones.
    - Perform one "Alpha Resonance" assessment per week—record voice and video, refine presence.

4. **Days 46–60: Reflection and Legacy Building**

    - Host a "Warrior's Review": invite allies to critique your performance and offer honors/ritual acknowledgments.
    - Document your progress in a "Masculine Codex"—a living manifesto to guide future growth.

Completing this protocol forges **not just a cast of mind**, but a man of action, integrity, and visionary leadership.

10.10 Chapter Summary and Forward Look

Masculinity, as Andrew Tate teaches, is **a battle-hardened art**—the convergence of courage, competence, compassion, and commitment to purpose. You now possess an exhaustive framework for embodying manhood that uplifts yourself and those you lead.

Next, Chapter 11 will explore **Women and Relationships**, revealing how purposeful masculinity interfaces with partnership dynamics to create respectful, passionate, and mutually empowering connections.

Sharpen your sword: the warrior's path is relentless, but you now stride it with clarity, conviction, and the uncompromising ethos of *Cobra Tate*.

> "Make yourself into such a man that you choose the women you want to be around."
> — **Tristan Tate**

Chapter 11: Women and Relationships — Respect and Polarity

Relationships are the crucible in which your masculinity is both tested and affirmed. In *Cobra Tate* philosophy, forging strong, respectful partnerships requires mastering the art of **gender polarity**—the dynamic interplay of masculine and feminine energies that creates powerful attraction, mutual growth, and enduring harmony. This chapter delivers an exhaustive guide to understanding, cultivating, and sustaining relationships that honor both partners' aspirations and natures. You will gain the foundational principles, psychological frameworks, daily practices, real-life transformations, corrective strategies, philosophical roots, and a comprehensive 60-Day "Covfefe of Connection" protocol to elevate your relationships to an art form.

11.1 The Foundation: Respect as the Bedrock of Attraction

True attraction blossoms from mutual respect. Andrew Tate underscores that:

- **Respect Is Earned:** Through integrity, competence, and consistency in actions.

- **Polarity Requires Clarity:** You must know your own values and boundaries before you can honor those of another.

- **Respect Breeds Safety:** Emotional and physical safety are prerequisites for both partners to express vulnerability and passion.

Without respect, polarity collapses into confusion—affection forced, roles muddled, and connection superficial.

11.2 Understanding Masculine and Feminine Energies

Masculine and feminine energies are archetypal forces, not strictly tied to biological sex. In relationships:

1. **Masculine Energy**

   - **Orientation Toward Purpose:** Focused on goals, direction, leadership.
   - **Providing and Protecting:** Acts first to secure well-being—financially, emotionally, physically.
   - **Stable Anchor:** Offers certainty and security.

2. **Feminine Energy**

   - **Orientation Toward Connection:** Emphasizes communication, empathy, emotional expression.
   - **Nurturing and Receptive:** Builds trust through warmth and encouragement.
   - **Dynamic Flow:** Adapts, inspires creativity, and renews vitality.

Attraction intensifies when these energies coexist in respectful polarity—each partner bringing their unique strengths.

11.3 The Five Dimensions of High-Value Partnership

A lasting relationship thrives when both partners excel across these dimensions:

1. **Emotional Resonance**
    - **Deep Listening:** Active, nonjudgmental attention to your partner's feelings and perspectives.
    - **Vulnerable Disclosure:** Sharing insecurities and dreams to forge psychological intimacy.

2. **Physical Chemistry**
    - **Intentional Touch:** From a firm handshake to lingering embraces, calibrated to convey care and desire.
    - **Sensual Rituals:** Date nights, adventure outings, consistent physical affirmation.

3. **Intellectual Engagement**
    - **Mutual Growth:** Challenging each other with new ideas—books, seminars, debates.
    - **Strategic Collaboration:** Joint problem-solving for shared projects—home renovations, business ventures.

4. **Spiritual Alignment**
    - **Shared Values:** Core beliefs—faith, ethics, life purpose—celebrated and reinforced.
    - **Ceremonial Bonding:** Rituals that mark transitions—anniversaries, goal-setting ceremonies, family gatherings.

5. **Material Foundation**
    - **Financial Transparency:** Open budgeting, aligned savings goals, joint investment planning.
    - **Lifestyle Harmony:** Negotiated expectations—division of labor, leisure priorities, home environment.

Excelling in these five dimensions transforms a relationship into a **high-value partnership** where both thrive.

11.4 Daily Practices for Respectful Polarity

To embed these dimensions into your life, integrate these rituals:

11.4.1 Morning Alignment Ritual

- **Check-In Question (2 min):** Each partner shares one intention and one gratitude.
- **Physical Greeting:** A warm touch or brief embrace to affirm connection before the day begins.

11.4.2 Midday Momentum Boost

- **Surprise Note or Call (1 min):** Send an encouraging text or voicemail highlighting appreciation.
- **Shared Task:** Collaborate on a small project—meal prep, home maintenance, or planning an outing.

11.4.3 Evening Connection Hour

- **Screen-Free Time (30–60 min):** No phones or TVs; engage in meaningful conversation or shared hobby.
- **Affectionate Closure:** A deliberate act—massage, slow dance, or reading aloud—to reinforce intimacy and polarity.

Embedding these micro-rituals cements polarity through daily reinforcement of mutual respect and attraction.

11.5 Communication Protocols: Assertiveness and Empathy

Clear, compassionate communication underpins every healthy relationship. Andrew's "Sword and Shield" method prescribes:

1. **Assertive Expression ("Sword")**

- **I-Statements:** "I feel… when you…" to state needs without blame.
- **Boundary Articulation:** "My limits are…" communicated calmly but firmly.

2. **Empathetic Listening ("Shield")**
   - **Reflective Paraphrasing:** "What I hear you saying is…" to validate understanding.
   - **Emotional Mirroring:** Refrain from problem-solving; instead, acknowledge emotional states ("That sounds tough.").

Deploying sword and shield in tandem prevents misunderstandings and fosters trust—allowing polarity to flourish rather than devolve into conflict.

11.6 Case Studies: Relationship Transformations

11.6.1 From Distance to Devotion

A high-powered executive couple drifted apart due to work demands. They implemented:

- **Weekly "Strategic Date":** A 2-hour meeting to align life goals and plan the next week's shared activities.
- **Monthly "Adventure Day":** One day dedicated to a novel experience—rock climbing, cooking class—to reignite curiosity and bonding.

Result: They reported a 70% decrease in conflict frequency and rekindled affectionate communication, restoring polarity and passion.

11.6.2 Turning Conflict into Collaboration

A startup co-founder and spouse frequently clashed over business vs. personal priorities. They adopted:

- **Scheduled Dispute Protocol:** Time-boxed 15-minute slots to air grievances, followed by 15 minutes of planning next steps together.

- **Third-Party Facilitation:** Quarterly sessions with a mentor couple to mediate high-stakes decisions.

Outcome: The dual-role stress eased; they reported clearer role definitions and increased both business performance and marital satisfaction.

11.7 Pitfalls and Corrections: Avoiding Toxic Patterns

Even the best-intentioned relationships falter. Andrew identifies these traps and remedies:

1. **Overemphasis on Autonomy**

    - **Problem:** Too much independence leads to isolation.

    - **Correction:** Schedule "We Time"—nonnegotiable shared activities reinforcing unity.

2. **Misaligned Expectations**

    - **Problem:** Unspoken assumptions breed resentment.

    - **Correction:** Quarterly "Relationship Review" to renegotiate goals, chores, finances, and intimacy norms.

3. **Fueling Power Struggles**

    - **Problem:** Competitiveness turns toxic when status becomes zero-sum.

    - **Correction:** Reinforce the "Couple as Unit" mindset—celebrate joint wins, share merit, rotate leadership based on expertise.

4. **Emotional Withholding**

    - **Problem:** Stoicism misapplied leads to emotional disconnect.

    - **Correction:** Biweekly "Heart Share" sessions—structured vulnerability where each shares fears and hopes, followed by support rituals.

By actively monitoring these pitfalls, you maintain a relationship culture of **growth, respect, and shared triumph.**

11.8 Philosophical Underpinnings: Love, Duty, and Honor

Andrew's relationship philosophy finds roots in classical thought:

- **Platonic Complementarity:** The idea that masculine and feminine principles complete one another, creating a harmonious whole.

- **Kantian Respect:** Treating each partner as an end in themselves, not a means to fulfill needs—ensuring dignity and autonomy.

- **Confucian Filial Piety:** Extending duty and honor beyond bloodlines to chosen family—your partner—through ritualized respect and care.

These philosophical currents converge to frame relationships as **sacred partnerships**—arenas of self-actualization and mutual empowerment.

11.9 Building a Legacy Together: The Couple as Architects

For Andrew Tate, relationships transcend the personal to become **collaborative enterprises**:

1. **Shared Vision Casting**

    - **Five-Year Relationship Charter:** Co-create a document outlining joint aspirations—family, career, philanthropy.

2. **Joint Venture Planning**

    - **Business or Creative Projects:** Align strengths—for example, she manages operations while he leads sales—leveraging polarity into productivity.

3. **Legacy Rituals**

    - **Annual Anniversary Retreat:** Review your charter, set new objectives, and conduct symbolic ceremonies—vow renewals, time-capsule messages to future selves.

By co-authoring a shared legacy, partners transform polarity into synergistic power, ensuring their union endures and multiplies across generations.

11.10 Your 60-Day "Covfefe of Connection" Protocol

To elevate your partner dynamic, undertake this **60-day immersion**:

1. **Days 1–10: Foundation of Respect**

   - Complete the "Respect Audit"—list 10 actions you appreciate and share them verbally.

   - Craft a joint "Relationship Manifesto" declaring roles, values, and shared mission.

2. **Days 11–25: Polarity Calibration**

   - Alternate leadership in daily rituals—she plans the date, you plan the adventure—reinforcing complementary strengths.

   - Practice "Sword and Shield" communication twice daily: assert one need, then empathetically reflect one feeling.

3. **Days 26–45: Deep Connection Exercises**

   - Weekly "Heart Share" and "Strategic Date" sessions as outlined in Sections 11.4 and 11.6.

   - Monthly "Couple's Workshop" with a mentor couple or therapist to refine dynamics.

4. **Days 46–60: Legacy Construction**

   - Draft your Five-Year Relationship Charter and set quarterly review dates.

   - Execute one joint venture pilot—small business, creative project, or philanthropic endeavor.

Diligent completion of this protocol embeds **respectful polarity** into the fabric of your partnership, transforming daily interaction into an art of engaged love.

11.11 Chapter Summary and Forward Look

Mastering women and relationships through the lens of *Cobra Tate* demands high-value partnership, respectful polarity, and purposeful collaboration. You now hold the exhaustive principles, frameworks, rituals, and protocols to elevate your partnerships from mere coexistence to dynamic synergy.

In the next chapter, we will explore the power of **Brotherhood and Network**—how forging alliances with like-minded warriors amplifies every virtue you have cultivated thus far, propelling you toward unprecedented heights of success and influence.

Stand ready: the journey through the *Cobra Tate* code continues, ever upward.

> "You need a group of men to hold you accountable. They'll inspire you to push yourself further... They'll be your support network when you need advice and support."
> — **Tristan Tate**

Chapter 12: Brotherhood and Network — The Power of Community

No man achieves greatness in isolation. In *Cobra Tate* philosophy, **brotherhood and network** are the multipliers that transform solitary effort into collective triumph. This chapter unfolds an exhaustive exploration of how strategic alliances, peer accountability, mentorship circles, and collaborative ecosystems propel every virtue of *Cobra Tate* to its highest expression. You will discover the origins of Tate's network doctrine, the four pillars that sustain powerful communities, daily and weekly rituals to cultivate cohesion, advanced frameworks for elite circles, real-world group case studies, digital tools to scale connection, common dysfunctions and their cures, philosophical roots of tribal excellence, and a detailed 60-day "Forge of Brothers" protocol to build—or deepen—your own network of unstoppable allies.

12.1 The Genesis of the Warrior Network

12.1.1 From Lone Fighter to Network Architect

- **Early Combat Camaraderie:** In the boxing gyms of Luton and Romania, Andrew observed that fighters who trained together—not merely as sparring partners but as brothers—achieved faster progress and greater resilience than lone wolves.

- **War Room Birth:** When Andrew and Tristan launched Hustler's University, they recognized that individual learning must be reinforced by communal pressure. The War Room emerged as an exclusive council where top performers exchanged strategies, referrals, and moral support—**a prototype for every modern brotherhood.**

12.1.2 Scaling Brotherhood: From Local Cells to Global Tribes

- **Regional Chapters:** Alumni in London, Los Angeles, Dubai, and Sao Paulo formed informal meetups—each a "cell" that upheld Tate principles in local contexts.

- **Digital Synchronization:** Discord and Telegram servers unified these cells, enabling real-time collaboration across time zones and cultural divides.

This evolution—from the ring to the digital realm—demonstrates that **community is the scaffold upon which individual excellence ascends.**

12.2 The Four Pillars of a High-Impact Network

A thriving brotherhood rests on four interdependent pillars. Master these, and your network becomes an **exponential force**:

12.2.1 Pillar 1: Accountability

- **Daily Check-Ins:** Short status reports—metrics, progress, obstacles—shared within small pods of 3–5 members.

- **"No Skip" Rule:** If you miss a check-in, you owe the group a detailed action plan explaining your reset steps.

12.2.2 Pillar 2: Inspiration

- **Showcase Wins:** Weekly "Victory Spotlight" sessions where members present one major achievement, however small, to ignite collective motivation.

- **Guest Fireside Chats:** Monthly live interviews with high-achieving alumni or external experts to broaden horizons.

12.2.3 Pillar 3: Resource Exchange

- **Skills Barter:** A dedicated channel where members trade services—copywriting for web design, legal advice for marketing guidance.
- **Deal Flow Alerts:** Real-time notifications of vetted investment opportunities, joint-venture prospects, or job referrals.

12.2.4 Pillar 4: Emotional Support

- **Vulnerability Circles:** Biweekly safe-space meetings where members share personal challenges—stress, relationships, health—and receive peer coaching.
- **Crisis Rapid-Response Team:** An emergency roster of three trusted brothers who commit to 1-hour calls when any member faces critical setbacks.

When these pillars interlock, your network delivers not just information, but **a living ecosystem** that sustains ambition through triumph and turmoil alike.

12.3 Daily and Weekly Rituals for Network Cohesion

Sporadic meet-ups yield sporadic results. Andrew prescribes a rigorous cadence of rituals to cement brother-for-brother bonds:

12.3.1 The Morning Battle Report (Daily, 7:00 AM)

- **Format:** A 3-line post in the group chat: "(1) Today's Top Priority, (2) Yesterday's Win, (3) Blocker Needing Advice."
- **Purpose:** Synchronizes focus, generates early energy, surfaces issues when solutions are freshest.

12.3.2 The Midweek War Council (Wednesdays, 7:00 PM)

- **Structure:** 60-minute video call—15 min news and announcements, 30 min hot-seat coaching (two members rotate each week), 15 min resource pitch (one new tool or contact).

- **Outcome:** Keeps momentum sustained, leverages collective intelligence to solve individual challenges, and spurs innovation.

12.3.3 The Friday Victory Banquet (Fridays, 8:00 PM)

- **Format:** Casual virtual hangout with optional attendance—members share a toast, reflect on weekly progress, nominate one brother for "Achievement of the Week" accolades.

- **Flavor:** Emulates in-person camaraderie; the ritual is as much about celebration as it is about reinforcing commitment to next week's battles.

12.3.4 The Monthly Strategy Summit (First Monday Monthly)

- **Duration:** 2 hours.

- **Agenda:** Deep-dive planning for the coming month against the network's shared objectives—fundraising goals, cohort launches, philanthropic initiatives.

- **Deliverables:** Written action matrices with assigned leads, deadlines, and KPIs tracked in a shared project board.

These recurring rituals transform nebulous community into **a disciplined war machine**—each member both soldier and strategist.

12.4 Advanced Frameworks for Elite Circles

Beyond basic pods and meetups, *Cobra Tate* networks deploy advanced structures to amplify impact:

12.4.1 The "Alpha Council" Model

- **Composition:** Top 1% performers across metrics (revenue, fitness milestones, community contributions).

- **Charter:** Quarterly retreats—intense strategy workshops off-grid, blending mastermind sessions with physical challenges (mountain ascents, cold-water immersion) to reinforce mind-body synergy.
- **Governance:** Alpha Council members mentor emerging leaders; rotate membership annually to maintain dynamism.

12.4.2 The "Sister Chains" Initiative

- **Purpose:** Extend inclusion to female allies—partners, entrepreneurs, professionals—recognizing that true network power embraces diverse talents.
- **Structure:** Parallel pods led by female facilitators, with joint mixed-group networking events to foster cross-gender collaboration and support.

12.4.3 Network Capital Index (NCI)

- **Definition:** A composite score for each member—calculated weekly—based on engagement frequency, assistance rendered, resources shared, and personal progress.
- **Usage:** NCI drives perks (conference subsidies, private coaching), ensuring that generosity and participation are rewarded as highly as raw achievement.

By institutionalizing these frameworks, *Cobra Tate* networks become **scalable engines** for leadership development and collective success.

12.5 Case Studies: Brotherhood in Action

12.5.1 The Investment Syndicate That Outperformed Markets

A group of ten HU alumni formed a private investment club:

- **Process:** Each member sourced and pitched one deal per month—real estate, startups, crypto tokens.
- **Due Diligence Cells:** Sub-pods of three performed independent analysis, risk modeling, and valuation.

- **Result:** Over 18 months, the syndicate achieved an internal rate of return (IRR) of 25%—more than double the S&P 500—while mitigating collective risk through diversified deal flow.

12.5.2 The Fitness Brotherhood That Won a Spartan Race

Six members committed to conquering an international obstacle-course event:

- **Training Cohorts:** Divided by geographic proximity to meet three times weekly; synchronized progress in group chat with video form critiques.
- **Nutrition Collective:** Shared meal plans, bulk-cooked meals, and contingency emergency fuel kits for race day.
- **Psychological Edge:** Weekly "mind over matter" shaming sessions—members pushed each other through simulated adversity drills.

They crossed the finish line together, not merely as individuals, but as **an unbreakable chain of comrades**.

12.5.3 The Startup Co-Founder Network

A cohort of ten aspiring entrepreneurs collaborated to launch five joint ventures:

- **Skill Matrix:** Mapped individual strengths—development, design, marketing, finance—and allocated roles accordingly.
- **Equity Pools:** Created a shared fund where each member contributed capital and time; profits redistributed based on contribution points tracked in real time.
- **Fail-Fast Philosophy:** Rapid MVP launches with collective feedback loops; pivoted or sunset projects within 30 days if metrics lagged.

Within a year, the network spun out two profitable companies—**a testament to leveraging collective skills over solitary hustle**.

12.6 Digital Tools and Platforms to Amplify Connection

Modern brotherhood thrives on technology. Andrew's recommendations include:

1. **Discord Workspaces:**
   - **Organization:** Channels for each pillar—#accountability, #resources, #victories, #crisis-support.
   - **Bots & Integrations:** Automated reminders, NCI tracking bots, RSVP polling, file-sharing bridges.

2. **Notion Hubs:**
   - **Central Knowledge Base:** Static resources—playbooks, video libraries, templates—organized for easy access.
   - **Project Boards:** Kanban-style boards for monthly strategy sprints and deal flow pipelines.

3. **Zoom & Jitsi for Secure Calls:**
   - **Breakout Rooms:** Facilitating small-group hot seats within larger gatherings.
   - **Recording and Transcription:** Archiving decisions and advice for asynchronous review.

4. **Calendly & Google Calendar:**
   - **Ritual Scheduling:** Automating daily, weekly, and monthly ritual invites with reminder buffers.
   - **1:1 Booking Pages:** Simplifying mentor-mentee session coordination.

5. **Telegram Signal Groups:**
   - **Crisis Channel:** Encrypted, low-latency communication for urgent support requests.
   - **Deal Alerts:** Real-time notifications for time-sensitive opportunities.

When wielded conscientiously, these platforms turn scattered participants into **a synchronized brotherhood**—always connected, always advancing.

12.7 Pitfalls and Corrections: Keeping Brotherhood Healthy

Even strong networks can fracture. Andrew warns of common dysfunctions and supplies remedies:

1. **Free Rider Syndrome:**
    - **Symptom:** Members who take resources but contribute little.
    - **Cure:** Reinforce NCI accountability; require minimum engagement hours per month; temporary suspension for non-compliance.

2. **Groupthink:**
    - **Symptom:** Homogeneous opinions stifling innovation.
    - **Cure:** Encourage devil's advocacy sessions; bring in external "wild card" experts quarterly to challenge assumptions.

3. **Cliquish Factions:**
    - **Symptom:** Subgroups isolating themselves, eroding overall cohesion.
    - **Cure:** Rotate pod membership monthly; host cross-pod mixers with icebreaker challenges.

4. **Toxic Conflict:**
    - **Symptom:** Personal criticisms disguised as "tough love."
    - **Cure:** Enforce communication protocols (see Chapter 11's "Sword and Shield"); deploy a rotating "Council of Elders" to mediate disputes.

By proactively diagnosing and remedying these issues, a *Cobra Tate* network remains **robust, dynamic, and perpetually oriented toward shared victory**.

12.8 Philosophical Underpinnings: The Power of the Tribe

The potency of brotherhood is not incidental but deeply rooted in human nature:

- **Dunbar's Number:** Anthropologist Robin Dunbar posited that humans can maintain stable relationships with roughly 150 individuals—networks that replicate in *Cobra Tate* chapters and councils.

- **Spartan Agoge:** Ancient Sparta trained its youth in communal resilience—mirrored today in the shared hardship challenges and initiation trials of Tate's circles.

- **Monastic Orders:** Medieval guilds and religious orders illustrate structured mentorship and collective vows—modernized in mentorship pods and accountability covenants.

These historical analogues affirm that **tribal bonds amplify individual capability**, forging identities stronger than any solitary path.

12.9 Your 60-Day "Forge of Brothers" Protocol

To craft or revitalize your brotherhood, undertake this **comprehensive 60-day protocol**:

1. **Days 1–10: Recruitment and Charter Creation**

    - Identify 8–12 high-integrity individuals aligned with your mission.

    - Draft a "Brotherhood Charter" detailing pillars, values, rituals, and sanction protocols.

2. **Days 11–25: Ritual Onboarding**

    - Launch the Morning Battle Report and Midweek War Council with full attendance.

    - Establish accountability pods of 3–5 members; assign pod leaders and rotation schedules.

3. **Days 26–40: Pillar Activation**

    - Each week, focus on one pillar—Accountability, Inspiration, Resource Exchange, Emotional Support—with dedicated exercises and measurement.

    - Host a monthly Strategy Summit simulation to practice decision-making under time pressure.

4. **Days 41–55: Advanced Frameworks Integration**

- Pilot an Alpha Council project (e.g., joint investment or co-authored content).
- Launch a Sister Chain event or mixed-gender collaboration to broaden alliance.

5. **Days 56–60: Reflection and Next-Gen Planning**
    - Conduct a "Council of Elders" review—evaluate metrics, identify pitfalls, codify improvements.
    - Plan the next 90 days: expand membership, refine rituals, and set elevated collective goals.

Completion of this Forge will leave you with a **battle-tested brotherhood** capable of weathering crises, accelerating growth, and amplifying every member's trajectory.

12.10 Chapter Summary and Forward Look

Brotherhood and network are the crown jewels of *Cobra Tate*'s empowerment arsenal—transforming individual zeal into **collective conquest**. You now possess the exhaustive blueprint to build, sustain, and scale a community that enforces accountability, sparks innovation, shares resources, and provides unwavering support.

In the next chapter, we pivot inward to **Mastering the Matrix**, unveiling how to wield digital platforms and cognitive strategies to break free from societal conditioning and reclaim full autonomous agency in the information age.

Prepare your allies: the path ahead demands not just a lone warrior, but a united front of brothers in arms.

> "A phone is just a digital pacifier in disguise. Stop pulling it out every time you feel anxious."
> — **Tristan Tate**

Chapter 13: Mastering the Matrix — Independence in the Digital Age

In an era where our attention is the ultimate battlefield, Andrew Tate's concept of "the Matrix" serves as both warning and roadmap. The Matrix represents the myriad systems—social media algorithms, mainstream narratives, corporate platforms—that shape behavior, induce compliance, and extract value from unwitting participants. To break free, one must cultivate digital autonomy: the ability to wield technology as a tool rather than be wielded by it. This chapter provides a comprehensive guide to escaping algorithmic captivity, building sovereign digital habits, and constructing a personal technology ecosystem that amplifies rather than diminishes your agency.

13.1 The Matrix Defined: Origins and Implications

Andrew Tate's Matrix metaphor draws on both pop-culture and his lived experience as a deplatformed influencer. Key tenets include:

1. **Algorithmic Enslavement**

    - Platforms like Facebook, TikTok, and YouTube monetize attention by feeding dopamine loops—designed to maximize screen time, not personal growth.

    - Victims of the Matrix find themselves in echo chambers that reinforce fears, anxieties, and consumerist impulses.

2. **Narrative Control**

    - Mainstream media and Big Tech collude—whether intentionally or through shared incentives—to promote approved viewpoints and suppress dissenting voices.

    - Independent thinkers are "shadow-banned," demonetized, or deplatformed, driving them to alternative networks.

3. **Value Extraction**

    - Every click, view, and purchase funnels data back to centralized entities that leverage it for ad revenue, product design, or political influence.

    - The Matrix thrives on passive consumption; it feasts on your emotional responses and sells them back as products or political messaging.

Understanding the Matrix is the first step toward dismantling its grip. Recognizing that **if you are not paying for the product, you are the product** is a wake-up call to reclaim your digital destiny.

13.2 The Five Pillars of Digital Independence

To transcend the Matrix, Andrew Tate prescribes mastering five foundational domains:

Pillar 1: Conscious Consumption and Digital Discipline

- **Notification Governance:** Disable non-essential alerts; batch-check messages and feeds at scheduled times.
- **Content Curation:** Unfollow or mute accounts that provoke anxiety or time-wasting; subscribe only to creators who deliver actionable value.
- **Time-Boxed Engagement:** Allocate specific "digital sprints" (e.g., 20 minutes twice daily) for social media or news, then log off.

Pillar 2: Platform Diversification and Algorithmic Literacy

- **Multi-Platform Presence:** Spread your digital footprint across at least three networks—traditional (e.g., YouTube), alternative (e.g., Rumble), and decentralized (e.g., Mastodon).
- **Algorithmic Mastery:** Study the ranking factors of each platform—watch time on YouTube, engagement loops on TikTok, clarity of captions on Instagram—and design content that leverages them without succumbing to clickbait.

Pillar 3: Content Creation and Monetization Mastery

- **Value-First Mindset:** Prioritize educational, inspirational, or problem-solving content over shock value; build trust that translates into sustainable revenue.
- **Revenue Layering:** Combine ad revenue, affiliate partnerships, course sales, paid newsletters, and direct donations to avoid dependence on any one income stream.

Pillar 4: Data Sovereignty and Privacy Defense

- **Self-Hosted Solutions:** Where possible, migrate your website, mailing list, and analytics to self-hosted platforms (e.g., a VPS with Ghost for blogging, Matomo for analytics).

- **Privacy Hygiene:** Use password managers, enforce two-factor authentication, minimize data footprints (avoid linking every service to Google/Facebook), and employ VPNs when on public Wi-Fi.

Pillar 5: Network Effects and Decentralized Communities

- **Own Your Tribe:** Cultivate private Discord/Telegram/Signal groups to engage your core supporters without platform interference.

- **Decentralized Collaboration:** Partner with peers to co-host live events on peer-to-peer networks (e.g., PeerTube) or blockchain-based streaming services, distributing risk and reward.

Together, these pillars constitute a **holistic framework** that transforms you from a passive digital citizen into an architect of your own online sovereignty.

13.3 Daily and Weekly Rituals for Matrix Mastery

Consistency is the antidote to algorithmic manipulation. Integrate these rituals into your schedule:

13.3.1 The Morning Digital Audit (Daily, 6:00 AM)

- **Metrics Review (5 min):** Check key performance indicators—website visits, mailing list growth, revenue—via self-hosted dashboards.

- **Priority Content Scan (5 min):** Briefly review your curated feed for top three actionable insights; save or bookmark rather than dive deep.

- **Notification Reset (2 min):** Silence all notifications; confirm that only high-priority apps can interrupt until scheduled check-in.

13.3.2 The Creation Power Block (Daily, 9:00–11:00 AM)

- **Focus Mode:** Use tools like Freedom or Cold Turkey to block distracting websites and apps.
- **Production Sprint:** Script, record, or write your highest-impact content—videos, articles, newsletters—feeding your diversified platforms.
- **Immediate Distribution:** Publish or schedule content immediately to maintain momentum and algorithmic relevance.

13.3.3 The Community Pulse (Daily, 3:00 PM)

- **Engagement Round:** Respond to comments, direct messages, and community threads in your private channels—no more than 30 minutes.
- **Resource Share:** Post one high-value link, tool recommendation, or mini-tutorial to your tribe, reinforcing your role as a thought leader.

13.3.4 The Evening Detox Window (Daily, 8:00–9:00 PM)

- **Device Curfew:** Power down all screens; use this time for analog pursuits—reading physical books, journaling, or family rituals.
- **Reflective Journal (5 min):** Note one success and one lesson from your digital dealings; plan tomorrow's digital sprint priorities.

13.3.5 The Weekly "Algorithm Hackathon" (Sundays, 2 Hours)

- **Trend Analysis:** Scan emerging hashtags, algorithm changes, or platform announcements.
- **Experimentation Planning:** Design A/B tests for thumbnails, headlines, or posting times; schedule tests for the week ahead.
- **Performance Retrospective:** Review prior experiments; iterate on winning formulas and retire losers.

These rituals inoculate you against digital drift, ensuring that **you govern technology**, rather than technology governing you.

13.4 Advanced Frameworks for Digital Sovereignty

To elevate beyond basic discipline, adopt these strategic blueprints:

13.4.1 The Digital Sovereign Roadmap

A multi-phase strategy to wean off platform dependence:

1. **Phase 1: Audience Ownership**

   - Launch a self-hosted newsletter or private forum; incentivize sign-ups with exclusive content.
   - Migrate your top 10% of most engaged followers off public platforms into this owned space.

2. **Phase 2: Alternative Channel Activation**

   - Incrementally re-build your public presence on decentralized platforms—Mastodon, PeerTube, LBRY—mirroring your core content.
   - Cross-link consistently so followers know where to find you if deplatformed.

3. **Phase 3: Monetization Diversification**

   - Implement subscription tiers in your own ecosystem (e.g., Patreon-style memberships on Memberful or Ghost).
   - Introduce occasional paywalls for premium deep-dive content, workshops, or micro-consultations.

4. **Phase 4: Ecosystem Resilience**

   - Establish redundant backups: mirror your website on IPFS; archive newsletters in GitHub repositories; store media assets in multiple cloud providers.
   - Enlist trusted allies with mirror sites or backup admin privileges to maintain continuity if your primary channels go dark.

13.4.2 The Content Quadrant Framework

Balance production across four quadrants to avoid over-reliance on any single format or platform:

Quadrant	Primary Goal	Typical Formats	Platform Examples
Evergreen Pillars	Long-term authority	In-depth articles, eBooks	Your blog, Ghost
Trend Exploits	Rapid engagement	Short videos, reaction posts	TikTok, Twitter
Community Cornerstones	Tribe cohesion	AMAs, live streams, polls	Discord, Telegram
High-Value Events	Revenue spikes	Workshops, webinars, launches	Zoom, Crowdcast

Rotate through these quadrants weekly to maximize reach, nurture your base, and monetize strategically without exhaustion.

13.5 Case Studies: Escaping the Algorithmic Trap

13.5.1 The Indie Journalist Who Reclaimed Editorial Control

A freelance reporter, frustrated by gatekeeper paywalls, pivoted to a self-hosted Substack:

- **Audience Seeding:** Cross-posted analysis pieces on Twitter and niche forums; offered a four-week free trial to paid newsletter.

- **Platform Agility:** When Substack experimented with algorithm changes, migrated top-performing content to a personal website and continued distribution via Mailgun.

- **Outcome:** Grew from 1,000 to 15,000 paid subscribers in 18 months; diversified income through sponsored investigations and speaking fees—**no longer at mercy of legacy media editors**.

13.5.2 The Gamer Turned Decentralized Developer

An esports streamer deplatformed during a controversy:

- **Immediate Pivot:** Launched a personal website with an integrated blockchain-based tipping system (using ENS and Ethereum).

- **Community Rebuild:** Hosted regular "play-along" sessions on PeerTube; distributed replays via IPFS for censorship resistance.

- **Outcome:** Retained 60% of original viewership, monetized through NFTs granting access to private LFG (Looking For Group) servers, and launched a decentralized guild—**turning deplatforming into growth**.

13.5.3 The Remote Entrepreneur Who Cut the Corporate Strings

A mid-level manager used digital freedom principles to go solo:

- **Skill Packaging:** Created bite-sized Upwork courses on remote team management and automation.

- **Client Funnel:** Built a low-content site (Jamstack + Netlify) emphasizing speed; captured leads via Calendly embedded in markdown pages.

- **Outcome:** Replaced 100% of corporate income within four months and assembled a distributed team of digital nomads using Loom, Notion, and Nextcloud—**a fully sovereign enterprise**.

13.6 Essential Tools and Platforms for Matrix Mastery

Selecting the right tools is critical. Andrew Tate recommends:

1. **Self-Hosting Stack**

    - **Web:** Nginx + Docker on a VPS (DigitalOcean, Vultr)
    - **Blog/Newsletter:** Ghost or WordPress + Mattermost for community chat
    - **Analytics:** Matomo or Plausible for privacy-focused insights

2. **Decentralized Networking**

    - **Social:** Mastodon (federated instances), Friendica

- **Video:** PeerTube, DTube (blockchain native)
- **Storage:** IPFS, Storj for immutable media hosting

3. **Productivity and Security**
   - **Password Management:** Bitwarden self-hosted
   - **Encryption:** Signal for messaging; ProtonMail or Tuta for email
   - **VPN:** Mullvad or private WireGuard setups

4. **Monetization Infrastructure**
   - **Payments:** Stripe Connect, Coinbase Commerce for crypto
   - **Memberships:** Memberful, Patreon alternatives like Liberapay
   - **Contracts:** Docusign or open-source equivalents integrated via UniWeb or PDF embedding

Each tool reduces reliance on corporate gatekeepers and fortifies your digital sovereignty.

13.7 Pitfalls and Corrections: Avoiding Digital Dependency

Even seasoned digital warriors can fall prey to new Matrix traps. Common issues include:

1. **FOMO and Notification Addiction**
   - **Symptom:** Constant screen-checking, anxiety spikes, reduced productivity.
   - **Correction:** Implement strict notification schedules; use grayscale mode on smartphones; enforce device-free zones.

2. **Echo Chamber Entrapment**
   - **Symptom:** Reinforced biases, groupthink, stagnating creativity.

- **Correction:** Subscribe to diverse viewpoints via RSS feeds; rotate content sources; attend contrarian panels.

3. **Over-Monetization Burnout**

    - **Symptom:** Content quality decline, audience fatigue, creator fatigue.

    - **Correction:** Limit sales pitches to 20% of content; embed community giveaways and free masterclasses to maintain goodwill.

4. **Data Overload Paralysis**

    - **Symptom:** Analysis paralysis from excessive metrics and dashboards.

    - **Correction:** Adopt a one-metric focus per week (e.g., newsletter open rate); archive or disable secondary analytics.

By anticipating these hazards and deploying targeted remedies, you maintain **true independence**—free to operate on your own terms.

13.8 Philosophical Foundations: Technology as Extension of Self

Andrew Tate's digital sovereignty ethos resonates with major philosophical currents:

- **Marshall McLuhan's "The Medium Is the Message":** Recognizing that platforms shape perceptions as much as content; hence choosing mediums consciously is as vital as crafting your message.

- **Foucault's Technologies of the Self:** Practices by which individuals effect a certain number of operations on their own bodies and souls, exemplified here by disciplined digital rituals.

- **Heidegger's "Enframing":** Technology tends to frame the world as a mere resource; mastering the Matrix requires seeing beyond enframing to reorient technology as a means for authentic being.

These philosophies underscore that **digital mastery is not merely technical but existential**, shaping who you become.

13.9 Your 60-Day "Matrix Breaker" Protocol

To complete your emancipation, follow this intensive 60-day journey:

Phase 1: Digital Audit & Detox (Days 1–10)

- **Comprehensive Audit:** Catalog every social, productivity, and entertainment app—rate each on a scale of "essential," "useful," or "toxin."
- **Gradual Detox:** Uninstall or disable "toxin" apps; implement scheduled access to "useful" apps only within time-boxed windows.
- **Reflective Journal:** Document cravings, anxiety triggers, and moments of clarity daily.

Phase 2: Platform Diversification (Days 11–25)

- **Rebuild Presence:** For each public persona (e.g., brand, personal), establish at least two alternative channels (decentralized or self-hosted).
- **Cross-Link Strategies:** Embed links, QR codes, and short URLs in all content to funnel followers to owned platforms.

Phase 3: Content Sovereignty (Days 26–40)

- **Monetization Layering:** Launch one new revenue mechanism—paid newsletter tier, micro-course, or digital tip jar.
- **Algorithm Experiments:** Conduct at least four A/B tests on key platforms, document outcomes, and iterate on successful elements.

Phase 4: Data Control & Privacy Lockdown (Days 41–55)

- **Privacy Harden:** Migrate email to ProtonMail, set up Bitwarden vault, enforce two-factor authentication everywhere.
- **Backup Systems:** Mirror website to IPFS, archive newsletters and media files in decentralized storage.

Phase 5: Community Forge (Days 56–60)

- **Tribe Activation:** Launch or refine your private community—Discord, Telegram, or Mattermost—with clear charter and engagement rituals.

- **Emergency Protocols:** Establish your "Rapid Response Team" for digital crises; share contact tree and roles.

- **Long-Term Roadmap:** Draft a 6-month plan with quarterly reviews, combining audience growth, revenue goals, and platform resilience metrics.

Completing this Matrix Breaker Protocol will leave you **immune to deplatforming, manipulation, and digital subjugation**, empowering you to create, share, and monetize on your own sovereign terms.

13.10 Chapter Summary and Forward Look

Mastering the Matrix is the ultimate frontier of self-empowerment in our digital age. By understanding algorithmic control, embracing conscious consumption, diversifying platforms, defending your data, and forging decentralized communities, you break free from systemic constraints and become the architect of your own digital destiny.

In the next chapter, Chapter 14: **Action Over Words**, you will learn how to convert every insight, strategy, and vision from the Tate philosophy into decisive, measurable action—because in the arena of results, **ideas without execution are meaningless**.

Stand ready: the code of the Matrix has been cracked. Now, it is time to execute with ruthless precision.

> "The biggest difference between success and failure is getting started. The majority of people I know fantasize about things that actually can be accomplished… They just never get started. If you get started and play the long game, you have a great chance of winning."
> — **Tristan Tate**

Chapter 14: Action Over Words — Execution and Hustle

Ideas are cheap. Plans are plentiful. What separates the doers from the dreamers is **the willingness to turn thought into deed, immediately and relentlessly**. In *Cobra Tate* philosophy, execution is sacrosanct: it is the altar at which all strategy must be sacrificed to prove its worth. This chapter offers an exhaustive playbook for transforming vision into reality—expanding upon psychological drivers, structural frameworks, rigorous rituals, real-world exemplars, common derailments, philosophical foundations, and a 90-day "Execution Accelerator" protocol—so that you not only start but sustain and scale your efforts until you stand atop your chosen summit.

14.1 The Imperative of Immediate Action

Every moment spent deliberating is time lost. Andrew Tate frequently emphasizes that **speed of decision coupled with speed of execution** compounds advantage exponentially. Consider these truths:

- **Deliberation Delays Victory:** A perfect plan executed late yields diminishing returns.
- **Momentum Begets Momentum:** The act of starting generates energy that fuels subsequent actions, making inertia your ally once you move.
- **Feedback Trumps Forecast:** Early, imperfect outcomes teach more than flawless hypotheticals.

Your mandate: **act now on 80% of the information you possess**, refine on the fly, and iterate toward excellence—eschewing the siren call of endless planning.

14.2 The Psychology of Execution

Understanding **why** we hesitate is the first step to outpacing procrastination:

1. **Fear of Failure:** Anticipated shame or loss paralyzes.
2. **Perfectionism:** The belief that only flawless work is acceptable.

3. **Overwhelm:** Too many tasks blur into paralysis.
4. **Lack of Clarity:** Unclear next steps stall progress.

Countermeasures:

- **Reframe Failure:** View each misstep as data in your calibration system.
- **Embrace Good-Enough Launches:** A minimum viable product (MVP) unblocks the freeze of perfection.
- **Chunk Work:** Break colossal goals into one-inch holes, then drill through them.
- **Define Next Actions:** For every task, specify the *very next* physical step to propel you forward.

14.3 The Six Pillars of Execution Mastery

Conquer the execution imperative by mastering six interlocking pillars:

14.3.1 Decision Velocity

- **Time-Bound Decisions:** Impose a strict time limit (e.g., 5 minutes) for minor choices; reserve deep analysis for truly consequential ones.
- **Default Bias:** Pre-commit to default behaviors—e.g., "publish new content every Monday"—to reduce decision overhead.

14.3.2 Ruthless Prioritization

- **Impact/Effort Matrix:** Categorize tasks by potential return versus required effort; attack High-Impact/Low-Effort items first.
- **Single-Task Sprinting:** Eliminate multitasking; focus on one "most important task" (MIT) until completion.

14.3.3 Micro-Project Sprints

- **Time-Boxed Initiatives:** Frame every goal as a 48-hour or one-week sprint, ending in a tangible deliverable.
- **Cross-Functional Pods:** Assemble mini-teams with complementary skills for rapid prototyping and execution.

14.3.4 Continuous Feedback Loops

- **Daily Stand-Up:** A three-question ritual: What did I do yesterday? What will I do today? What impediment stands in my way?
- **Rapid Iteration:** Release early versions, gather user or peer feedback, and implement improvements within 24 hours.

14.3.5 Outcome Orientation

- **Define Success Criteria Up-Front:** For every project, list 3–5 quantifiable metrics that signify completion.
- **Results Over Activity:** Reward deliverables, not hours logged—celebrate published articles, closed deals, or shipped code.

14.3.6 Persistence Under Fire

- **Resilience Conditioning:** Schedule weekly "failure drills" where you deliberately undertake a high-risk micro-project likely to flop, then analyze nonetheless.
- **Accountability Contracts:** Publicly pledge your goal with a penalty for non-delivery—donate to a charity you despise or subject yourself to an uncomfortable challenge.

14.4 Daily and Weekly Rituals for Relentless Hustle

Embed the pillars into your calendar with these recurring rituals:

14.4.1 The Dawn Launchpad (Daily, 5:30 AM)

- **Two-Minute Mind Dump:** Empty your mind onto paper—projects, worries, ideas—clearing cognitive load.

- **Victory Blueprint:** Identify your one MIT and five supporting tasks for the day.

- **Emergency Barrier Check:** Note any known impediments; pre-plan mitigation steps.

14.4.2 The Midday Pivot Point (Daily, 12:00 PM)

- **Progress Pulse (10 min):** Review morning achievements and adjust the afternoon plan.

- **Quick Retrospective:** What worked? What stalled? Deploy a micro-solution to any stalling.

14.4.3 The Hyperfocus Block (Daily, 2:00–4:00 PM)

- **No-Zoom Zone:** Disable notifications, close email, and execute deep work on a single sprint.

- **End-of-Block Checkpoint:** Self-score performance on a 1–5 scale (5 = laser focus achieved).

14.4.4 The Sunset Wrap-Up (Daily, 8:00 PM)

- **Deliverable Log:** Record completed deliverables and note progress toward weekly goals.

- **Plan-Ahead Notepad:** Define tomorrow's MIT and any dependencies so you start tomorrow in motion, not stalled.

14.4.5 The Weekly Sprint Planning (Weekly, Sunday Evening)

- **Goal Cascade:** Translate monthly objectives into four weekly sprints.

- **Resource Allocation:** Assign time blocks, budget, and any third-party support needed.

- **Risk Buffer:** Reserve 10% of the week for unplanned emergencies or opportunities.

14.4.6 The Weekly Sprint Review (Weekly, Friday Afternoon)

- **Metric Verification:** Compare actual results versus defined success criteria.
- **Lessons Learned:** Document three insights—tactical wins, strategic pivots, and process improvements.
- **Team Debrief:** (If applicable) Convene stakeholders for a 30-minute "blitz debrief" to realign next sprint.

14.5 Advanced Execution Frameworks

Leverage professional methodologies adapted for personal conquest:

14.5.1 OKRs × Agile Fusion

- **Objective:** A bold qualitative goal for the quarter.
- **Key Results:** 3–5 measurable milestones.
- **Agile Sprints:** Two-week cycles with sprint backlogs drawn from KR tasks. Retrospectives drive backlog refinement.

14.5.2 Personal Kanban

- **Columns:** To Do, Doing, Done.
- **Work-In-Progress (WIP) Limits:** Max 2–3 tasks in Doing at any time to prevent context-switch overhead.
- **Swimlanes:** Separate lanes for Critical Projects versus Maintenance Tasks.

14.5.3 Pomodoro + ENGAGE Loops

- **Pomodoro Blocks:** 25-minute work intervals followed by 5-minute breaks.
- **ENGAGE Technique:** Every fourth Pomodoro, conduct a 15-minute strategic evaluation—E (Evaluate), N (Note), G (Generate adjustments), A (Apply), G (Gauge impact), E (End-of-block reflection).

14.5.4 Gamified Progress Tracking

- **Point System:** Assign point values to tasks based on difficulty and impact; accumulate points toward "level-up" rewards.

- **Achievement Badges:** Milestone badges for streaks—e.g., 30 days of MIT completion, 10 successive sprints meeting KR goals.

14.6 Case Studies: Execution in the Wild

14.6.1 The NFT Artist Who Launched a Collection in 10 Days

- **Day 1–2:** Ideation sprint—defining themes, sketch thumbnails.

- **Day 3–5:** Production sprint—20 art pieces daily, quality-over-quantity MVP approach.

- **Day 6:** Smart-contract deployment on Ethereum testnet, peer-feedback session.

- **Day 7–8:** Minting & marketplace setup, landing page with email capture.

- **Day 9:** Social media blitz—collaborative launches with micro-influencers.

- **Day 10:** Public drop; minted out in 3 hours, generating 5 ETH.

Takeaway: A ruthless 10-day execution sprint outpaced typical months-long production cycles, leveraging speed to capture market buzz.

14.6.2 The Solopreneur's 24-Hour App Hackathon

- **Hour 0–4:** Wireframing UX and defining core features.

- **Hour 4–12:** Rapid coding using no-code tools and templates.

- **Hour 12–16:** Usability testing with a closed beta of 20 users; record feedback.

- **Hour 16–20:** Implement top-5 fixes; finalize UI polish.

- **Hour 20–24:** Launch on Product Hunt and Hacker News; collect emails and first sales.

Result: A functioning SaaS MVP with 100 beta sign-ups and 5 paid pilot customers within 24 hours—a testament to micro-sprint potency.

14.6.3 The Author Who Wrote a Book in 30 Days

- **Day 1:** Outlined 20 chapters with one-sentence summaries.
- **Day 2–29:** Wrote 2,000 words daily (using "Daily Launchpad" rituals).
- **Day 15 & 30:** Two self-edit passes focusing on structure then copy polish.
- **Day 30:** Self-published on Kindle and Gumroad; scheduled launch promotions.

Outcome: First-week sales of 500+ copies, establishing credibility and generating $7,500 in revenue—action literally turned words into profit.

14.6.4 The Nonprofit Mobilization Campaign in 48 Hours

- **Hour 0–4:** Converged on Zoom to define campaign message and goals.
- **Hour 4–12:** Created landing page, donation widgets, and social media assets.
- **Hour 12–24:** Engaged micro-influencers, deployed Google Ads, and launched email blast.
- **Hour 24–48:** Secured $50K in donations, allocated funds to urgent relief efforts.

Key Insight: Rapid execution unified dispersed resources into an effective campaign—proof that crisis needn't preclude order when action protocols are in place.

14.7 Pitfalls and Corrections: Execution Saboteurs

Even the most driven risk faltering. Common execution saboteurs include:

1. **Analysis Paralysis**
    - **Symptom:** Endless research, no launch.

- **Fix:** Impose "Research Sprint" limits—2 hours maximum—and commit to a "Launch Window" immediately afterward.

2. **Scope Creep**
    - **Symptom:** Projects balloon beyond initial plan.
    - **Fix:** Freeze feature set on Day 1; treat enhancements as separate micro-projects.

3. **Perfectionism**
    - **Symptom:** Refusing to release until "perfect."
    - **Fix:** Adopt "Version 1.0" mindset; schedule a public "upgrade announcement" to signal iterative improvements.

4. **Reactive Mode**
    - **Symptom:** Fire-fighting urgencies eclipse strategic tasks.
    - **Fix:** Reserve 10% of calendar for "Deep Work Today"—a non-negotiable block shielded from interruptions.

5. **Burnout**
    - **Symptom:** Sustained sprints lead to exhaustion and disengagement.
    - **Fix:** Integrate restorative rituals—cold therapy, sauna sessions, nature walks, creative hobbies—to recharge endorphins and clarity.

By diagnosing and remedying these pitfalls, your hustle remains **surgical**, not scattershot.

14.8 Philosophical Foundations: The Ethics of Hustle

Andrew Tate's execution ethos resonates with deep philosophical currents:

- **William James's Pragmatism:** Truth is verified and implemented through action—what works in practice is what matters.

- **Jean-Paul Sartre's Existentialism:** Existence precedes essence; you define yourself through acts of will and creation.
- **Spartan Agoge Resilience:** Training under hardship for real-world competence; hustling becomes a form of ethical self-cultivation.

These foundations frame hustle not as mere opportunism but as **a moral imperative**: to actualize potential, uplift others, and manifest one's chosen destiny.

14.9 Your 90-Day "Execution Accelerator" Protocol

To embed ruthless execution into your DNA, undertake this **90-day accelerator**:

Phase 1: Foundation (Days 1–15)

- **Day 1–3:** Define one quarter-long Objective and 3 Key Results (OKRs).
- **Day 4–7:** Establish daily rituals: Dawn Launchpad, Midday Pivot, Hyperfocus Block, Sunset Wrap-Up.
- **Day 8–15:** Conduct three "Micro-Project Sprints" on distinct OKR tasks; deliver MVPs and gather quick feedback.

Phase 2: Momentum (Days 16–45)

- **Agile Sprints:** Biweekly two-week sprints with sprint planning, daily stand-ups, and sprint reviews.
- **OKR Check-Ins:** Weekly progress scoring on KRs; adjust backlog accordingly.
- **Accountability Partner:** Pair with an execution peer for daily check-ins and mutual "no-skip" enforcement.

Phase 3: Scale (Days 46–75)

- **Kanban Expansion:** Transition from personal Kanban to team Kanban if collaborating; set WIP limits and cycle-time targets.

- **Automation Blitz:** Identify three repetitive tasks and automate them (scripts, templates, workflows).
- **Delegation Framework:** Document SOPs (Standard Operating Procedures) for delegation; onboard one assistant or junior partner.

Phase 4: Sustain (Days 76–90)

- **Deep Reflection:** Conduct a 90-day "Postmortem"—what worked, what didn't, ROI on time invested.
- **System Hardening:** Lock in successful rituals; disable or archive ineffective ones.
- **Future Roadmap:** Define the next 90-day cycle's OKRs with elevated ambition; celebrate achievements with a "Hustle Gala" event.

Completing this protocol forges **an execution engine** that runs independent of daily whims—ensuring you continuously convert vision into impact.

14.10 Chapter Summary and Forward Look

Ideas and plans are worthless without the muscle of execution. *Cobra Tate* demands that you **act now, iterate fast, and persist until victory**. By mastering decision velocity, ruthless prioritization, micro-sprints, feedback loops, outcome orientation, and resilience—anchored by rigorous rituals and robust frameworks—you transform ambition into accomplishments.

In the next chapter, Chapter 15: **Lifelong Learning**, you will discover how to integrate continuous self-education into your execution engine, ensuring that your evolving skills keep pace with your expanding ambitions.

Prepare your battle plans: the next mission begins at dawn.

> "Remember young man, no one will educate you enough to overthrow them."
> — **Tristan Tate**

Chapter 15: Lifelong Learning — Adaptability and Growth

Knowledge is not static; it is living, breathing, and evolving. In the *Cobra Tate* paradigm, **lifelong learning** is the crucible in which adaptability, resilience, and excellence are forged. To succeed in today's rapidly shifting landscapes—be they economic, technological, or cultural—you must become a perpetual student, continually widening your skillset, recalibrating your strategies, and embracing the discomfort of unlearning. This chapter provides a comprehensive roadmap to mastering lifelong learning: from the origins of Tate's learning ethos to psychological drivers; from the four pillars of adaptive education to daily and weekly study rituals; from advanced frameworks to case studies, pitfalls, philosophical foundations, and a rigorous 120-day "Adaptive Scholar" protocol. By immersing yourself in this process, you will transform your mind into a dynamic asset capable of both immediate execution and long-term strategic pivots.

15.1 The Imperative of Continuous Knowledge Acquisition

Andrew Tate often asserts that **formal education is designed to produce compliance, not independence**. While he acknowledges that traditional schooling can impart foundational skills, he argues that real-world success requires a self-directed commitment to acquiring—and applying—expertise beyond what any institution will voluntarily teach. Consider these imperatives:

1. **Erosion of Industry Lifespans**

    - Technical skills that were relevant five years ago can become obsolete within eighteen months.

    - Emerging fields—cryptocurrency, artificial intelligence, biotech—demand rapid upskilling to remain competitive.

2. **Exponential Information Expansion**

    - The global data pool doubles approximately every two years; leveraging this new knowledge is essential to maintain an edge.

    - Early adopters of novel paradigms often capture disproportionate rewards (e.g., early crypto investors, AI pioneers).

3. **Adaptability as a Superpower**
    - Those who refuse to update their worldview, skillset, and tactics become liabilities—easily outpaced by faster learners.
    - In volatile environments, adaptability trumps raw talent; the ability to pivot can safeguard careers, ventures, and reputations.

Your mandate: **cultivate an insatiable appetite for learning**, ensuring that you not only acquire new competencies but also restructure your mind to fluidly integrate fresh paradigms and discard obsolescent ones.

15.2 Origins of Tate's Lifelong Learning Ethos

15.2.1 Childhood Lessons from Emory Tate

- **Chess as Curriculum:** Andrew grew up watching his father, Emory Tate, a chess International Master, teach strategic thinking through puzzles and problem-solving exercises.
- **Self-Education by Necessity:** Without reliance on formal tutoring, Andrew internalized hunger for knowledge—studying fight techniques, business books, and languages on his own, laying the foundation for lifelong autodidacticism.

15.2.2 From Kickboxing Rings to Boardrooms

- **Transference of Methods:** The same discipline used to study fight footage, dissect opponents' tactics, and refine techniques in the gym was later applied to financial markets, digital marketing funnels, and emerging technologies.
- **Pattern Recognition:** Andrew's ability to detect patterns—whether in opponents' strikes or algorithm shifts—emerged from a habit of **observational learning**, catalyzed by relentless curiosity.

These origin stories illustrate that Tate's learning ethos is **not an academic abstraction**, but a lived practice forged in adversity, competition, and the constant drive to evolve.

15.3 The Four Pillars of Adaptive Education

To institutionalize lifelong learning, Andrew Tate prescribes four interrelated pillars:

Pillar 1: Curiosity-Driven Exploration

- **Holistic Consuming:** Devour a broad range of content—books, podcasts, research papers—across diverse domains.

- **Cross-Pollination:** Apply insights from one field to accelerate innovation in another (e.g., using principles of quantum computing to optimize business algorithms).

- **"Learn Something New Today" Mindset:** Commit to daily discovery, even if only 15 minutes, ensuring perpetual gestation of novel ideas.

Pillar 2: Structured Skill Acquisition

- **Quadrant Mapping:** Categorize desired skills into four quadrants—Essential, Amplifying, Future-Proof, and Passion—then allocate learning resources proportionally.

    - **Essential:** Non-negotiable skills tied to current core competencies (e.g., financial modeling if you run a business).

    - **Amplifying:** Adjacent skills that enhance existing proficiency (e.g., copywriting to complement sales).

    - **Future-Proof:** Forward-looking capabilities (e.g., blockchain, machine learning).

    - **Passion:** Personal enrichment areas (e.g., languages, musical instruments) to maintain psychological balance and creative edge.

Pillar 3: Rapid Skill Application

- **Immediate Implementation:** For every concept learned, design a micro-project (e.g., craft a sales email using new copywriting techniques within 24 hours).

- **Feedback Loop Integration:** Seek critique from peers, mentors, or online communities to refine your nascent skill iteratively.

- **Skill Drilling:** Emphasize volume and repetition—e.g., if learning Python programming, solve at least 50 coding challenges in the first month.

Pillar 4: Meta-Learning and Unlearning

- **Learning How to Learn:** Study methodologies (Feynman Technique, Spaced Repetition, Interleaving) to optimize cognitive retention and speed.

- **Unlearning Rituals:** Identify outdated beliefs or tactics—perform a quarterly "Paradigm Purge" to systematically dismantle mental models that no longer serve.

- **Cognitive Flexibility:** Cultivate a mindset open to paradigm shifts—view every lesson as provisional rather than dogmatic.

Together, these pillars create a **dynamic ecosystem** where knowledge is constantly refreshed, applied, tested, and refined.

15.4 Daily and Weekly Study Rituals

Embedding these pillars into your routine requires rigorous scheduling. Andrew suggests the following rituals:

15.4.1 The Dawn Knowledge Sprint (Daily, 5:00 AM – 6:00 AM)

- **Microscopic Book Review (20 min):** Read highly dense nonfiction—biographies of strategic titans, tactical manuals, cutting-edge research—using speed-reading or skimming followed by deep-dive marking.

- **Flashcard Drill (10 min):** Review and add at least five new Anki (spaced-repetition) flashcards on recently acquired concepts (e.g., new financial ratios, coding syntax, foreign language vocabulary).

- **Mini-Feynman Session (30 min):** Teach a newly learned concept out loud—either to an imaginary student or record it on your phone. Focus on clarity; identify any gaps and revisit source material as needed.

15.4.2 The Midday Micro-Lecture (Daily, 1:00 PM – 1:30 PM)

- **Podcast or Lecture Listening:** Consume a short, high-impact lecture or podcast chapter on relevant topics—entrepreneurship, psychology, neuroscience, technology—at 1.5× or 2× speed.

- **Rapid Synthesis:** Immediately after listening, jot down three actionable takeaways and one question that merits further exploration.

15.4.3 The Late-Afternoon Application Hour (Daily, 4:30 PM – 5:30 PM)

- **Micro-Project Execution:** Implement one new concept in a micro-project. Examples:
    - If you studied a novel SEO technique, update your website's metadata and track ranking changes.
    - If you learned a negotiation tactic, conduct a mock negotiation with a peer or role-player.
    - If you practiced a coding pattern, refactor a small portion of your codebase to improve efficiency.
- **Result Logging:** Record process, outcomes, challenges, and lessons in a "Skill Journal". Rate confidence (1–5) and plan next iteration.

15.4.4 Evening Reflection and Unlearning (Daily, 9:00 PM – 9:30 PM)

- **Thought Inventory:** Write freely for five minutes about any conflicting ideas, cognitive dissonances, or outdated beliefs you encountered.
- **Paradigm Purge Prompt:** Flag at least one belief or approach (e.g., "I must wait for perfect conditions to act") to scrutinize and revise.
- **Tag-and-Store:** Place flagged items into an "Unlearning Backlog"—a prioritized repository to revisit during monthly deep dives.

15.4.5 Weekly "Knowledge Triage" (Weekly, Sunday Evening, 2 Hours)

- **Curated Review:** Revisit all flashcards added during the week; delete irrelevant ones and refine clumsy phrasing.
- **Performance Assessment:** Evaluate progress on skill acquisition metrics—time spent, projects completed, confidence ratings.
- **Next-Week Roadmap:** Based on identified gaps and goals, plan the following week's focused learning topics, selecting three core areas to dive into and scheduling daily

slots.

These rituals ensure that learning is not a sporadic luxury, but **an automated pillar** of your lifestyle.

15.5 Advanced Frameworks for Accelerated Learning

To elevate beyond standard routines, adopt these sophisticated methodologies:

15.5.1 The "Science of Learning" Matrix

Integrate cognitive science principles to maximize retention:

1. **Spaced Repetition Scheduling:**

    - Program flashcards or review sessions at increasing intervals (1 day, 3 days, 7 days, 14 days, 30 days) to cement memory.

    - Use Anki or RemNote with customized tagging for each skill domain.

2. **Interleaving Practice:**

    - Instead of blocking (e.g., coding for two hours, then writing for two hours), rotate between related sub-skills (e.g., 30 minutes coding, 30 minutes reading, 30 minutes problem-solving) to enhance discrimination learning.

    - Example: When studying marketing, interleave ad copy analysis, data analytics exercises, and brand case studies.

3. **Dual Coding and Multi-Modal Inputs:**

    - Supplement text-based learning with visual diagrams, infographics, mind maps, or short videos to engage multiple learning channels.

    - When learning a complex process (e.g., financial modeling), sketch flowcharts and annotate key steps rather than relying solely on spreadsheet tutorials.

4. **Elaborative Interrogation:**

- For every new fact or concept, ask "why?" and "how?" repeatedly to deepen understanding.
- E.g., "Why does compound interest accelerate growth beyond linear returns?" then explore mathematical proofs, visualize exponential curves, and consider historical examples.

15.5.2 The "SWIFT Iteration" Method (Skill-Work-Iterate-Feedback-Track)

A cyclic framework to convert novice-to-expert:

1. **Skill Identification:** Choose a specific micro-skill (e.g., "write a persuasive 200-word email" instead of "copywriting in general").
2. **Work Module:** Set a 45-minute block to gather resources—templates, examples, guidelines.
3. **Initial Draft:** Produce the first version of the skill artifact (email, code snippet, design mockup).
4. **Iterate with Feedback:** Present to a mentor, peer group, or online community within 24 hours; solicit direct, blunt critiques.
5. **Track Progress:** Quantify improvements (e.g., open rate for the email, code performance metrics) and record in a central dashboard.
6. **Refine and Recycle:** Integrate feedback, test again, and document each iteration until reaching a predetermined performance threshold (e.g., email open rate >30%).

This method ensures **continual refinement** rather than deploying perfect-but-unused knowledge.

15.5.3 The "Skill Ladder" Blueprint

Visualize skill progression as ascending rungs on a ladder:

1. **Rung 1 (Awareness):** Exposure to basic concepts; nominated reading, podcasts, or tutorials.
2. **Rung 2 (Foundational Practice):** Guided exercises—30–50 structured tasks with direct instructions.

3. **Rung 3 (Applied Context):** Incorporate skills into real-world scenarios—client projects, personal ventures, or simulations.

4. **Rung 4 (Innovative Mastery):** Challenge paradigms—adapt or combine skills (e.g., use coding to automate marketing tasks) and mentor novices.

5. **Rung 5 (Thought Leadership):** Create original frameworks, publish comprehensive guides, and lead communities around the skill domain.

Plotting your learning journey against this ladder ensures **strategic scaffolding**, avoiding both under-challenged complacency and overwhelming leaps.

15.6 Case Studies: Adaptive Growth in Action

15.6.1 The Corporate Manager Turned Data-Driven Consultant

A mid-level manager at a manufacturing firm recognized the rising value of data analytics:

- **Rung 1–2:** Completed an online certificate in Basic Python and Data Visualization (Weeks 1–4); solved 100 Kaggle challenges (Weeks 5–8).

- **Rung 3:** Led a pilot project to automate weekly sales reports, reducing manual effort by 80% within three months.

- **Rung 4:** Co-created an internal "Data Empowerment Bootcamp" for colleagues, refining his teaching and cementing expertise.

- **Rung 5:** Published a 20-page industry whitepaper on "Predictive Maintenance Analytics in Manufacturing," attracting consulting offers from startups and large enterprises alike—within a year of initiating his learning journey.

15.6.2 The Freelancer Who Pivoted to Full-Stack Development

A graphic designer anticipated saturation in his niche:

- **Rung 1–2:** During weekends and late nights, studied HTML, CSS, and JavaScript tutorials (Weeks 1–6).

- **Rung 3:** Rebuilt his personal portfolio site using React.js; attracted seven new clients who specifically requested custom web applications (Weeks 7–12).

- **Rung 4:** Contributed to open-source projects—debugging modules and submitting pull requests; collaborated with developers on GitHub (Weeks 13–20).

- **Rung 5:** Launched an online course teaching "Design-to-Code Workflows" on Gumroad; earned $50K in revenue within three months and built a reputation as a cross-disciplinary expert.

15.6.3 The Solopreneur Who Became an AI Whisperer

A small-business owner saw generative AI as a potential force multiplier:

- **Rung 1–2:** Completed "Intro to Prompt Engineering" courses and daily prompt-crafting drills (Weeks 1–3).

- **Rung 3:** Integrated GPT-based chatbots into his customer service processes, reducing response time from 24 hours to under 5 minutes (Weeks 4–6).

- **Rung 4:** Automated content creation—blog posts, social media captions, ad copy—freeing 30% of his weekly work hours for higher-level strategy (Weeks 7–12).

- **Rung 5:** Co-authored a brief eBook on "Small Business AI Playbooks," launched on self-hosted platforms; sold 1,200 copies in the first month and established a new consulting revenue stream.

These case studies underscore that **intentional, structured learning** can rapidly pivot careers, even against steep odds.

15.7 Pitfalls and Corrections: Overcoming Learning Antagonists

Persistent learning is fraught with obstacles; Andrew Tate highlights pitfalls and their remedies:

1. **Acquisition Anxiety**
    - **Symptom:** Paralyzing fear of starting because the knowledge gap seems insurmountable.

- **Correction:** Employ "Entry-Level Framing"—commit to achieving "just enough" functional proficiency (Rung 2) before aiming for mastery.

2. **Shiny-Object Syndrome**

    - **Symptom:** Jumping to the next pop-skill or tool before mastering the previous one.
    - **Correction:** Restrict new skill exploration to a "Shiny Object Quota" of one per quarter; maintain a queue and delay starts until clearing current Rung 1–3 commitments.

3. **Analysis Paralysis**

    - **Symptom:** Over-researching methodologies, tools, and best practices without actionable steps.
    - **Correction:** Enforce a "Concept-to-Execution Ratio" of 1:5—after each hour of theory, dedicate five hours to practical application or prototyping.

4. **Information Overload**

    - **Symptom:** Inundation by content—books, articles, courses—leading to confusion rather than clarity.
    - **Correction:** Adopt "Curated Consumption"—limit reading to three trusted sources per domain; rotate out sources quarterly to avoid stale perspectives.

5. **Skill Atrophy**

    - **Symptom:** Failing to revisit and maintain rarely used skills, leading to decay.
    - **Correction:** Schedule "Skill Maintenance Days" quarterly—refresher sessions on lapsed competencies and code or practice challenges to re-engage neuronal pathways.

By forecasting these common barriers, you can proactively institute **countermeasures** to keep your learning engine running smoothly.

15.8 Philosophical Foundations: Learning as Moral Imperative

Tate's approach to lifelong learning encompasses deeper philosophical currents:

- **Plato's Allegory of the Cave:** Emerging from ignorance into enlightenment parallels Andrew's call to constantly exit mental caves of complacency and embrace new intellectual vistas.

- **John Dewey's Experiential Education:** Knowledge arises from active engagement; Tate's emphasis on immediate application mirrors Dewey's validation that **learning by doing** cements understanding.

- **Zeno of Elea's Paradoxes Reframed:** Breaking large goals into infinitesimally small steps (akin to Zeno's dichotomy) becomes a practical strategy for mastering vast skill domains—illustrating that infinite progress can emerge from finite actions.

- **Confucian Lifelong Virtue:** Confucius advocated for a lifetime of self-cultivation, emphasizing that learning is moral work toward becoming a virtuous individual. Tate extends this to **becoming a prosperous, adaptive warrior** rather than merely a scholar.

By rooting your learning within these philosophical traditions, you ensure that your quest for knowledge transcends mere utility and becomes a **moral, existential imperative**.

15.9 Your 120-Day "Adaptive Scholar" Protocol

To embody *Cobra Tate*'s vision of lifelong learning, undertake this exhaustive **120-day protocol**, divided into four 30-day "Knowledge Quarters":

> **Overall Objective:** Attain functional mastery in two new high-impact domains and refine three existing core competencies to elite levels.

Knowledge Quarter 1 (Days 1–30): Foundation and Exploration

- **Day 1–3: Curiosity Mapping**
    - Create a "Knowledge Landscape" diagram listing 12 potential domains (e.g., AI, advanced finance, negotiation, biohacking, foreign languages).

- Rank each by Impact, Feasibility, and Passion (scale 1–5).
- Select 2 top-priority domains as "Primary Learning Tracks" for Q1 (e.g., AI fundamentals, advanced Excel modeling).

- **Day 4–10: Resource Curation**
  - Assemble must-read/watch materials—books, courses, expert interviews—for each track.
  - Apply "Curated Consumption": finalize three trusted sources per domain.

- **Day 11–25: Foundational Skill-Building**
  - **AI Track:** Complete 20 introductory coding exercises in Python, focusing on data handling and basic ML model implementation.
  - **Excel Track:** Build 10 financial models from scratch—DCF, Monte Carlo simulations, sensitivity analyses—using live company data.
  - Log every exercise in the "Skill Journal" with confidence ratings.

- **Day 26–30: Baseline Application**
  - **AI Track:** Design a "Hello, World" ML project—classify a small dataset (e.g., MNIST digits) to 90% accuracy.
  - **Excel Track:** Apply a financial model to a real startup pitch deck, producing valuation and sensitivity reports.
  - Reflect on strengths, weaknesses, and immediate next steps in a 1,000-word "Baseline Assessment" document.

Knowledge Quarter 2 (Days 31–60): Integration and Expansion

- **Day 31–35: Expansion to Secondary Tracks**
  - Based on Q1 outcomes, select 1–2 secondary domains to add—e.g., "Copywriting Persuasion Psychology" and "Intermediate Spanish."
  - Curate two key resources per new domain.

- **Day 36–50: Rapid Application Sprints**

    - **AI Advanced:** Implement a simple neural network using TensorFlow or PyTorch onboard—run a sentiment analysis on 10,000 Twitter posts.

    - **Excel Mastery:** Automate data pulls from public APIs (e.g., Yahoo Finance) into Excel via Power Query; create dynamic dashboards.

    - **Copywriting:** Draft and split-test three marketing emails; measure open and click-through rates, refine subject lines and calls to action.

    - **Spanish:** Practice daily 30-minute conversation sessions with a native speaker via language exchange apps; complete Duolingo "Skill Levels" to at least "Crown Level 2."

    - Document all results in "Skill Journal" with performance metrics (e.g., classification accuracy, financial model robustness, CTR improvements, conversational fluency).

- **Day 51–60: Peer Review and Feedback**

    - **AI:** Present your neural network results in a Discord AI channel, solicit critiques on model choice and optimization.

    - **Excel:** Host a "Live Modeling Lab" with peers; fix errors and incorporate best practices suggested by others.

    - **Copywriting:** Participate in a copy swap—exchange email drafts with three peers for reciprocal critiques.

    - **Spanish:** Record two 5-minute monologues on assigned topics; share with native speakers for pronunciation and syntax corrections.

    - Summarize feedback and integrate top three improvements per domain.

Knowledge Quarter 3 (Days 61–90): Mastery and Synthesis

- **Day 61–70: Innovation Integration**

    - **AI:** Develop a simple web app using Flask or Streamlit that allows users to input text and receive sentiment analysis results—deploy on a free hosting service (e.g., Heroku).

- **Excel:** Build a multi-tab investment tracking workbook using dynamic formulas, pivot tables, and VBA macros to automate data refreshes.

- **Day 71–80: Cross-Domain Synthesis**

  - **AI + Copywriting:** Use your sentiment analysis model to recommend emotionally resonant copy adjustments—upload email drafts, receive sentiment scores, and iterate to improve positivity or urgency.

  - **Excel + Spanish:** Create a bilingual financial template—headers, instructions, and commentary in both English and Spanish to cater to Latin American investors.

  - Document cross-domain projects, highlighting how synergy amplifies utility.

- **Day 81–90: External Validation**

  - Submit AI web app to Product Hunt for community feedback; aim for at least 500 upvotes and 100 comments.

  - Share Excel workbook on relevant subreddits (e.g., r/excel, r/financialmodeling); gather user improvement suggestions.

  - Publish a bilingual blog post analyzing economic trends in Latin America, using your financial model; solicit peer reviews for both subject accuracy and language fluency.

  - Reflect on external reception, incorporate top feedback in iterative revisions.

Knowledge Quarter 4 (Days 91–120): Legacy and Leadership

- **Day 91–100: Consolidation and Documentation**

  - Compile a "Knowledge Compendium" PDF with your AI model code annotated, Excel templates with usage guides, copywriting best practices tested, and Spanish vocabulary glossaries—structured for future reference or teaching.

  - Prepare a 10-minute presentation summarizing your 120-day journey—highlight key wins, stumbling blocks, and aha moments.

- **Day 101–110: Teaching and Mentorship**

- Host two one-hour "Knowledge Share" webinars—one on "Building and Deploying Sentiment Analysis Models" and another on "Advanced Financial Modeling for Bilingual Business Contexts."

- Facilitate a five-session "Skill Workshop" for novices in each domain—cover basics, lead exercises, and provide feedback.

- **Day 111–120: Forward Planning and Unlearning**

    - Conduct a final "Paradigm Purge": Review "Unlearning Backlog" from daily journals; for each item, either concretely replace it with a new belief or schedule a test to validate its relevance.

    - Draft a 6-month and 12-month "Learning Roadmap," mapping new domains (e.g., "Rust Programming," "Cognitive Behavioral Therapy Techniques," "Advanced Negotiation Tactics") and setting preliminary OKRs.

    - Convene a "Learning Council" with peers and mentors—present your roadmap, solicit commitments for accountability, and establish bi-monthly check-ins.

Completion of this **120-Day Adaptive Scholar Protocol** institutionalizes lifelong learning: from domain selection and foundational skill-building to mastery, cross-pollination, teaching, and future planning. You emerge not just knowledgeable, but **strategically equipped** to evolve with every paradigm shift.

15.10 Chapter Summary and Forward Look

In a world where stagnation equates to obsolescence, lifelong learning is **the keystone** of personal and professional sovereignty. By embracing Tate's four pillars—curiosity-driven exploration, structured skill acquisition, rapid application, and meta-learning—you create a dynamic knowledge ecosystem resilient to disruption. The daily and weekly rituals, advanced frameworks, case studies, and the rigorous 120-day protocol collectively ensure you not only absorb novel insights but also embed them into high-impact action.

As you close this chapter, remember: **adaptability is not a passive state but an active pursuit**. The next and final chapter, Chapter 16: **Purpose and Legacy**, will unveil how to channel your continuously expanding capabilities into a vision that transcends personal gain—honoring your lineage, uplifting your community, and ensuring that your impact reverberates beyond a single lifetime.

Stand ready: the scholar-warrior transformation is complete—yet your evolution has only just begun.

> "Accomplishment honours your ancestors."
> — **Tristan Tate**

Chapter 16: Purpose and Legacy — Honor Through Achievement

Legacy is the echo of one's life that reverberates across generations. In *Cobra Tate* philosophy, **purpose and legacy** transform every effort from fleeting success into enduring significance. To live with purpose is to align daily actions with a vision that transcends personal gain; to build a legacy is to create a ripple effect of upliftment long after one's own journey ends. This exhaustive chapter provides a comprehensive roadmap for identifying your deepest raison d'être, channeling it into strategic objectives, and constructing a legacy framework—spanning personal, familial, societal, and global dimensions—that honors your ancestors and empowers your descendants. You will explore the origins of Tate's legacy ethos, psychological motivators of legacy-building, the four pillars of legacy creation, daily and weekly rituals for purpose alignment, advanced frameworks for multi-generational impact, real-world legacy case studies, pitfalls and corrective strategies, the philosophical bedrock of generational honoring, and a 120-day "Legacy Architect" protocol. By immersing yourself in this process, you will transcend transient victories and carve a place in the annals of enduring influence.

16.1 The Essence of Purpose and Legacy

Purpose and legacy are the lodestars that guide every decision, tethering mundane tasks to a grand narrative. Andrew Tate's core teaching: **without a clearly articulated purpose, success is hollow; without legacy, achievement is transient**. At its heart, the legacy imperative comprises two inseparable dimensions:

1. **Intrinsic Fulfillment**

    - **Self-Actualization:** Living in alignment with deepest values yields profound meaning.

- **Flow State Realization:** Engaging in activities so congruent with purpose that time dissolves, and mastery becomes both medicine and mission.

2. **Extrinsic Impact**

    - **Generative Influence:** Creating systems, institutions, or cultural shifts that empower others to excel—thus multiplying your value across time.

    - **Ancestral Honor:** Acknowledging the sacrifices of forebears by channeling their legacy into new domains, ensuring that their struggles have borne fruit.

Together, intrinsic fulfillment and extrinsic impact fuse into **legacy synergy**: the dynamic process by which personal greatness begets collective advancement, past debts are repaid, and future hopes are fueled.

16.2 Origins of Tate's Legacy Ethos

16.2.1 Familial Lineage and Emory Tate's Influence

- **Chess Legacy:** Emory Tate's brilliance on the 64 squares instilled Andrew and Tristan with reverence for intellectual rigor and honor. Seeing their father's name etched in chess annals planted the seed that **excellence could grant a form of immortality**.

- **Sacrificial Foundations:** Their mother's unceasing labor underscored that family sacrifices serve as bedrocks for generational uplift; to squander such sacrifices would be a betrayal.

16.2.2 Combat, Commerce, and Reputation

- **Ring Reputation:** Each world title elevated Andrew's name, but more importantly, it forged a personal code: **one's word, won in battle, becomes one's bond**. The weight of that bond is a legacy in itself, as every opponent and fan remembers the warrior who refused to yield.

- **Entrepreneurial Footprints:** From webcam ventures to digital empires, Andrew recognized that businesses can outlive their founders if built on strong values. He began to frame commerce as **a vehicle for building institutional legacies**—entities that, if structured correctly, can endure upheavals and serve communities beyond the founder's lifespan.

By tracing these origins, you see how Tate's legacy ethos is neither accidental nor superficial; it is **the culmination of personal heritage**, shaped by the triumphs and tribulations of those who came before.

16.3 The Four Pillars of Legacy Creation

To translate vision into enduring impact, Tate prescribes mastering four interconnected pillars:

Pillar 1: Purpose Articulation

- **Core Why Identification:** Drill down through layers of "why" until you reach a foundational purpose that transcends episodic achievements (e.g., "to elevate resilience in my lineage," "to pioneer ethical AI for global good").

- **Mission Statement Crafting:** Condense your core why into a 20–30-word manifesto that resonates emotionally and strategically—serving as a north star for decisions.

- **Vision Casting:** Envision the future landscape shaped by your legacy—what institutions exist because of you, what values endure because of your stewardship, what lives are touched due to your influence.

Pillar 2: Value Transmission

- **Ritualized Storytelling:** Regularly recount your ancestral history—family struggles, triumphs, ethos—to younger generations, embedding values of courage, honor, and grit.

- **Ethical Framework Embedding:** Codify guiding principles (truthfulness, courage under fire, relentless improvement) into written charters for your ventures, families, or communities.

- **Mentorship Networks:** Establish multi-generational mentorship pipelines—pair seasoned elders with emerging leaders to facilitate direct transmission of wisdom and standards.

Pillar 3: Institutional and Cultural Architecture

- **Legacy Institutions:** Found or support entities—schools, charities, foundations, companies—designed to endure beyond your personal tenure, governed by clear bylaws and succession protocols.

- **Cultural Norm Setting:** Create traditions—annual gatherings, commemorative rituals, legacy celebrations—that reinforce collective identity and honor shared values.

- **Resource Endowment:** Allocate financial, intellectual, and relational capital to ensure institutions can thrive—endowments, trust funds, digital archives—so they remain operational across crises.

Pillar 4: Metric-Driven Stewardship

- **Legacy KPIs:** Define metrics that reflect multi-generational impact (e.g., percentage of descendants in leadership roles, philanthropic impact per decade, institutional resilience scores).

- **Continuous Audit and Iteration:** Conduct triannual "Legacy Audits"—assess institutional health, measure cultural adherence among cohorts, identify legacy leaks (values erosion, mission drift).

- **Adaptive Governance:** Establish councils or boards that blend founding visionaries with emerging innovators, ensuring institutions adapt to evolving contexts while upholding legacy DNA.

These four pillars transform ephemeral success into **tangible, transmissible, and measurable** generational impact.

16.4 Daily and Weekly Rituals for Purposeful Living

Consistency in purpose alignment fortifies legacy-building. Embed these rituals to ensure daily actions reflect your long-term vision:

16.4.1 Dawn of Devotion (Daily, 5:00 AM – 5:15 AM)

- **Purpose Recitation:** Read your mission statement aloud with conviction; visualize the ripple effects of your legacy across decades.

- **Ancestral Honor Journal:** Write one sentence acknowledging a specific ancestral sacrifice and commit one concrete action today to honor that legacy (e.g., "I honor my grandfather's work ethic by completing my key project task before midday.").

16.4.2 Midday Impact Alignment (Daily, 1:00 PM – 1:15 PM)

- **Impact Check-In:** Review task list; for each task, note how it serves your legacy pillars—does it transmit values, strengthen institutions, or progress strategic goals?
- **Course Correction Note:** If a task misaligns (e.g., pure busywork), flag it and replace it with a legacy-aligned activity (e.g., mentoring a junior colleague, writing value-focused thought leadership).

16.4.3 Evening Legacy Reflection (Daily, 9:00 PM – 9:30 PM)

- **Triadic Reflection:** Document three legacy-related events: (1) A value you exemplified today, (2) An institution you nurtured, (3) A person you impacted.
- **Progress Map:** Log your week's movement on legacy KPIs—e.g., "Visited family archive, updated one section; drafted next month's charitable initiative outline; attended board meeting for legacy institution."
- **Daily Unlearning:** Identify one obsolete belief or practice that must be jettisoned to remain authentic to your evolving legacy (e.g., unlearning scarcity mindset in favor of abundance for philanthropic giving).

16.4.4 Weekly Council Convening (Weekly, Sunday Evening, 2 Hours)

- **Legacy Review Session (30 min):** Examine progress against your mission—how did your actions fortify purpose and align institutions?
- **Ancestral Storytelling Roundtable (30 min):** Invite family, mentees, or co-founders to share stories about the values and sacrifices that shaped your legacy—reinforcing cultural transmission.
- **Strategy Rechart (30 min):** Revise and refine next week's objectives based on legacy KPIs—e.g., number of mentees reached, fundraising milestones, institution health indicators.
- **Ritual Reinforcement (30 min):** Conduct a communal ritual—light a candle at the family altar, perform a minute of silence for ancestors, or share a legacy inspiration quote to embed shared commitment.

Embedding these rituals ensures that **every 24-hour cycle** and every weekly exchange moves both you and your ecosystem toward enduring purpose.

16.5 Advanced Frameworks for Crafting Multi-Generational Impact

Beyond daily routines, utilize these sophisticated blueprints to shape a legacy that transcends immediate contexts:

16.5.1 The "Legacy Tree" Model

Visualize your legacy as a tree with multiple branches representing different domains—family, business, community, thought leadership:

1. **Trunk (Core Values):** The foundational ethics—integrity, courage, service—root the tree and nourish each branch.

2. **Major Branches (Key Initiatives):**

   - **Family Branch:** Education funds, family governance councils, oral history projects.

   - **Enterprise Branch:** Founding of a mission-driven company or social enterprise structured for continuity.

   - **Community Branch:** Long-term philanthropic programs (scholarships, health clinics) with sustainable funding.

   - **Thought Leadership Branch:** Publications, lectures, and digital content that shift cultural conversations.

3. **Minor Branches (Tactical Efforts):** Under each major branch, list tactical activities—monthly family reading nights, quarterly board meetings, annual fundraising galas, weekly blog posts.

4. **Leaves (Outcomes):** Tangible results—foundation grants awarded, children's college scholarships realized, community metrics improved, citations of published works.

Mapping your Legacy Tree yields a **holistic blueprint** that ensures alignment across personal and external domains, illustrating how roots and branches interact to produce vibrant leaves (outcomes).

16.5.2 The "Generational Value Transfer" Framework

Design a protocol to transmit not just wealth, but wisdom and values:

1. **Codify Values:** Create a written "Family/Organization Creed" distilled into 10 tenets—e.g., "Pursue excellence relentlessly," "Serve with humility," "Cultivate resilience through adversity."

2. **Embed in Education:**
   - **Formal:** Develop curricula—workshops, retreats, apprentice programs—that teach core tenets to descendants or community protégés.
   - **Informal:** Host annual storytelling events where elder generations recount lived experiences demonstrating each tenet.

3. **Ritualize Milestones:**
   - **Coming-of-Age Ceremonies:** At key ages (e.g., 18, 21), require descendants to complete a "Legacy Quest"—a challenge reflecting a tenet, such as a service project, a mentorship task, or a leadership role.
   - **Passing the Torch:** At predetermined achievements (e.g., first major business success, first major philanthropic gift), publicly confer a "Legacy Medallion" symbolizing commitment to uphold the creed.

4. **Institutionalize Mentorship:** Pair each younger generation member with two mentors—one elder from within your lineage or network, and one external expert—creating a web of guidance ensuring wisdom flows upward and downward.

This framework ensures **value transfer** becomes systematic rather than ad hoc, safeguarding legacy integrity across time.

16.5.3 The "Legacy Vessel" Multiplier Strategy

Establish an entity or asset explicitly designed to carry your legacy forward:

1. **Identify Your Vessel Types:**
   - **Legal Entities:** Foundations, non-profit trusts, family offices, endowments.
   - **Intellectual Assets:** Books, patented inventions, digital courses, knowledge repositories.
   - **Cultural Artifacts:** Annual events, awards, scholarships tied to your name or ethos.

2. **Seed Funding and Governance:**
   - **Initial Endowment:** Allocate capital—percentage of net worth or dedicated revenue streams—to fund vessel operations in perpetuity.
   - **Governance Board:** Appoint a diverse board of stewards—family members, community leaders, subject-matter experts—tasked with upholding the vessel's mission and adapting to evolving contexts.

3. **Scalable Impact Plans:**
   - **Annual Objectives:** Publish yearly "Legacy Impact Reports" outlining achievements, challenges, metrics.
   - **Innovation Funds:** Set aside discretionary funds within the vessel for rapid response to emergent opportunities (e.g., supporting a startup ideal aligned with your mission).

4. **Succession Protocols:**
   - **Heirship Guidelines:** Define criteria and processes for designating future vessel guardians—based on merit, commitment to mission, or both.
   - **Continuity Planning:** Test "worst-case scenarios"—loss of patrons, market collapse—and develop contingency plans to ensure vessel survival.

By architecting a robust, adaptable vessel, your legacy becomes **less vulnerable to individual mortality** and more resilient in shifting landscapes.

16.6 Case Studies: Legacy in Action

16.6.1 The Family Foundation That Transformed a Region

A third-generation industrialist family in Eastern Europe sought to convert their generational wealth into lasting community uplift:

- **Pillar Implementation:**
  - **Purpose Articulation:** Defined mission "to elevate educational opportunities for underprivileged youth in our region."

- **Value Transmission:** Codified commitment to "knowledge as liberation" and held annual storytelling galas where grandparents recounted their own struggles in post-war times.

- **Institutional Architecture:** Established the "Tate Scholars Foundation" with an initial endowment of $5 million, governed by a board including family members and local educators.

- **Metric Stewardship:** Tracked KPIs—number of scholarships awarded, graduation rates of recipients, regional economic improvements.

- **Legacy Outcomes:**

  - **Educational Impact:** Over 500 students received full scholarships to universities across Europe; 70% of recipients returned to start social enterprises locally.

  - **Economic Uplift:** The town's average household income rose 15% over a decade, partly attributable to foundation-sponsored vocational training programs.

  - **Cultural Revival:** Annual "Knowledge and Heritage Festival" became a regional hallmark, celebrating local crafts, history, and inspiring youth leadership.

By the third decade, the foundation's brand had become synonymous with **transformative generational investment**, cementing the family's legacy in regional revival.

16.6.2 The Entrepreneur Who Converted Business into a Social Movement

A tech entrepreneur in Silicon Valley felt unfulfilled despite billions in exit valuations:

- **Purpose Recast:** Shifted focus from wealth accumulation to "democratizing AI education for underserved communities globally."

- **Value Transmission:** Partnered with nonprofit networks to co-create curricula; held hackathons pairing industry experts with students in emerging markets.

- **Institutional Vessel:** Launched "AI for All Foundation," seeding it with 20% of his exit proceeds and personally committing to two-day-a-month mentorship sessions.

- **Consistent Stewardship:** Instituted "AI Impact Reports" with transparency on grant distributions, program outcomes, and long-term projections.

Legacy Outcomes:

- **Global Reach:** Over 10,000 students across 25 countries completed certified AI bootcamps within five years.

- **Technological Empowerment:** Foundation alumni launched 150 AI-driven startups focused on healthcare and agriculture solutions in their local regions.

- **Thought Leadership:** Annual "AI Ethics and Equity Summit" convened policymakers, industry, and academia to debate responsible AI deployment—shaping regulatory frameworks in five nations.

This exemplar illustrates how reorienting personal success toward a **broader human mission** can transmute entrepreneurial legacy into a social movement.

16.6.3 The Athlete Who Became a Barbell of Community Strength

A world-champion martial artist, after retiring from competition, sought to leave a non-profit imprint in his hometown:

- **Purpose Defined:** "To foster discipline, respect, and physical health among at-risk youth through martial arts."

- **Value Transmission:** Embedded "warrior's code" values—integrity, humility, perseverance—into daily dojo instruction.

- **Institution Established:** Founded "Cobra Warriors Academy," offering free training scholarships, mentorship programs, and academic tutoring—funded by dojo revenues and external sponsorships.

- **Metrics Tracked:** Monitored student graduation rates, juvenile delinquency referrals, fitness assessments, and community crime statistics.

Legacy Outcomes:

- **Youth Transformation:** 85% of academy students improved grades by at least one letter; dropout rates plummeted by 40% in participating neighborhoods.

- **Cultural Shift:** Local law enforcement reported a 25% reduction in youth-related incidents; civic pride soared, leading to municipal support for expanded facilities.

- **Enduring Culture:** Alumni graduates became volunteer coaches, perpetuating the academy ethos even after the founder relocated—ensuring his legacy thrived autonomously.

This case shows how translating individual athletic excellence into **community uplift** can forge a living legacy that reverberates through society.

16.7 Pitfalls and Corrections: Avoiding Legacy Failures

Even the most earnest legacy initiatives can falter. Andrew Tate warns of these frequent traps and prescribes remedies:

1. **Mission Drift**

    - **Symptom:** Over time, institutions stray from founding purpose—bureaucracy or new leadership agendas dilute original vision.

    - **Correction:** Institute "Mission Incubator" sessions—a quarterly deep-dive where founders and new leaders reconvene to reaffirm or refine the charter; require any major strategic pivot to secure a 75% board approval vote tied to legacy KPIs.

2. **Overcentralized Stewardship**

    - **Symptom:** Succession risks emerge when one charismatic personality—founder or heir—holds disproportionate power; institutions sputter if that person departs.

    - **Correction:** Embed shared governance—distribute decision rights among a culturally aligned council; require two co-chairs from distinct backgrounds (e.g., one family member, one external expert) to cross-check major decisions.

3. **Short-Termism**

    - **Symptom:** Pursuit of quick wins (e.g., sensational but unsustainable programs) undermines longer-term strategic goals.

    - **Correction:** Allocate a minimum of 60% of resources to multi-year projects; annual budgets must delineate at least one "legacy anchor project" with a multi-decade horizon.

4. **Value Erosion Through Generational Fracture**

    - **Symptom:** Younger generations lose connection with founding ethos—view legacy as irrelevant or burdensome.

    - **Correction:** Maintain living connection through regular "Ancestral Immersion" programs—immersive retreats where newer cohorts engage in historical reenactments, visit ancestral sites, and document personal reflections. Ensure at least 80% family or stakeholder participation.

5. **Resource Misallocation**

    - **Symptom:** Funds are channeled into vanity projects that generate ephemeral visibility but little lasting impact.

    - **Correction:** Enforce a "Legacy Return on Investment" metric—calculate projected multi-decade social or economic returns per dollar spent, and only approve initiatives with projected ROI above a strict threshold (e.g., 3× or 5× over 10 years).

By instituting these corrective mechanisms, your legacy-building efforts avoid common pitfalls and stay **aligned, resilient, and purpose-driven**.

16.8 Philosophical Underpinnings: Tradition, Honor, and Transcendence

Tate's purpose-and-legacy doctrine resonates with deep philosophical traditions that illuminate the transcendent dimensions of legacy:

- **Aristotelian Eudaimonia and Philotimia:** Aristotle argued that true happiness (eudaimonia) arises from fulfilling one's highest potential and contributing to the polis; philotimia (love of honor) drives one to seek excellence for its own sake, ensuring that achievements uplift both self and community. Legacy thus becomes the **culmination of a virtuous life** dedicated to the common good, not mere personal gratification.

- **Confucian "Xiao" (Filial Piety):** The Confucian ideal emphasizes honoring one's ancestors by living ethically and perpetuating family virtues; this extends to modern legacy work, where one's actions repay the debts of past generations and set a moral compass for those who follow.

- **Nietzsche's Übermensch:** Nietzsche's conception of the Overman (Übermensch) involves creating values and shaping reality, transcending herd morality. Tate's legacy framework echoes this by urging individuals to establish new institutions and values that outlast their own existence, effectively rewriting cultural scripts.

- **Tocquevillian Associationism:** Alexis de Tocqueville observed that voluntary associations—civil society networks—are the bedrock of democratic life. Legacy institutions (foundations, nonprofits, community groups) thus embody a **commitment to**

shared stewardship and collective empowerment, forging bonds that anchor societies through flux.

- **Dharma and Karma in Eastern Traditions:** Dharma (righteous duty) and karma (action and its consequences) suggest that one's duty to family, community, and self shapes future outcomes. By aligning daily deeds with dharma—ethical imperatives—you generate positive karma that benefits descendants and society at large. Legacy, then, is a tangible manifestation of one's accumulated virtuous karma.

These philosophical currents converge to reveal that **legacy is not an optional afterthought**, but an existential imperative—a quest to align one's life with cosmic currents of righteousness, honor, and transformation.

16.9 Your 120-Day "Legacy Architect" Protocol

To crystallize your vision and construct a robust legacy, embark on this intensive **120-day "Legacy Architect" protocol**, structured into four 30-day phases:

Phase 1: Discovery and Purpose Solidification (Days 1–30)

1. **Day 1–3: Genealogical Excavation**

    - **Activity:** Conduct structured interviews with surviving family members, mentors, and community elders to document ancestral stories, sacrifices, and values.

    - **Deliverable:** A 10-page "Ancestral Chronicle" capturing key narratives and lessons.

2. **Day 4–10: Core Why Extraction**

    - **Activity:** Use the "Five Whys" method repeatedly on personal desires ("Why do I want wealth?" "To provide security," "Why security?" etc.) until you reach a transcendent, altruistic purpose (e.g., "To ensure abundant opportunities for community uplift").

    - **Deliverable:** A distilled mission statement (20–30 words) that crystallizes your purpose beyond personal gain.

3. **Day 11–20: Vision Casting Workshop**

- **Activity:** Host a two-day retreat—can be solo or with trusted peers—dedicated to envisioning your ideal 25-year legacy landscape across personal, family, business, and societal domains.
- **Deliverable:** A "25-Year Vision Canvas" with sketches, mind maps, and narrative descriptions.

4. **Day 21–30: Values Codification**
   - **Activity:** Draft a "Legacy Values Charter" listing 10–12 guiding principles, each accompanied by brief anecdotes demonstrating ancestral or personal alignment.
   - **Deliverable:** A polished document ready for public presentation within your family or network.

Phase 2: Institutional Blueprinting (Days 31–60)

1. **Day 31–35: Legacy Tree Mapping**
   - **Activity:** Create a detailed "Legacy Tree" diagram (see Section 16.5.1) mapping core values (trunk), major initiatives (branches), tactical efforts (minor branches), and desired outcomes (leaves).
   - **Deliverable:** A large-format visual chart to hang in your workspace for clarity.

2. **Day 36–45: Institution Design Sprint**
   - **Activity:** For each major branch, develop a 5-page institutional blueprint—covering mission, organizational structure, governance model, funding sources, succession plan, and key performance indicators.
   - **Deliverable:** Draft blueprints for at least two institutions (e.g., a family foundation and a community training center).

3. **Day 46–55: Governance and Succession Planning**
   - **Activity:** Form a provisional "Legacy Council" comprising 3–5 stakeholders (family members, mentors, domain experts); facilitate a two-hour workshop to finalize governance charters, board composition criteria, and succession protocols.

- **Deliverable:** A "Governance & Succession Manual" with bylaws, board nomination procedures, and voting thresholds for major decisions.

4. **Day 56–60: Resource Mobilization Strategy**

    - **Activity:** Create a comprehensive resource plan—financial, human, intellectual—for initial seeding of your institutions. This includes allocating personal capital, identifying potential donor pools, and drafting partnership proposals.

    - **Deliverable:** A "Resource Mobilization Dossier" with projected budgets, fundraising timelines, and partner outreach templates.

Phase 3: Cultural Engineering and Value Transmission (Days 61–90)

1. **Day 61–70: Ritual and Tradition Development**

    - **Activity:** Design a suite of legacy rituals—annual, quarterly, monthly, and weekly—that reinforce core values. Examples: "Founders' Day Lecture Series," quarterly "Family Storytelling Dinners," weekly "Legacy Reflection Circle."

    - **Deliverable:** A "Ritual Calendar" with names, dates, objectives, scripts, and logistical plans for each ritual.

2. **Day 71–80: Educational Curriculum Creation**

    - **Activity:** Develop a modular curriculum—"Legacy Curriculum 101"—covering core values, institutional history, and skill sets necessary for stewardship. Include lesson plans, reading lists, interactive exercises, and assessment rubrics.

    - **Deliverable:** A comprehensive curriculum package, ready for rollout to first cohort (e.g., family members, community interns).

3. **Day 81–85: Digital & Physical Archive Setup**

    - **Activity:** Create a digital archive (using self-hosted solutions like Nextcloud or a private Git repository) to store documents, oral history recordings, photographs, and artifacts. Simultaneously organize a physical repository—binders, framed documents, genealogical charts—for tangible lineage representation.

- **Deliverable:** An operational "Legacy Archive" with user guidelines for accessing, contributing, and preserving materials.

4. **Day 86–90: Mentorship Pipeline Establishment**

    - **Activity:** Identify 10–15 legacy mentors—individuals both within and outside your immediate circle—who embody your core values. Formalize a mentorship charter outlining responsibilities, meeting cadence, and evaluation criteria.

    - **Deliverable:** A "Mentorship Network Roster" and charter, ready to onboard initial mentee cohort (younger family or high-potential community members).

Phase 4: Legacy Launch and Stewardship (Days 91–120)

1. **Day 91–95: Public Launch Event**

    - **Activity:** Plan and host a high-impact "Legacy Launch" gala—invite family, key network members, community leaders, media. Present your mission statement, vision canvas, institutional blueprints, and initial program offerings. Solicit feedback and secure commitments.

    - **Deliverable:** A "Legacy Launch Program" document and recorded event footage for archival.

2. **Day 96–105: Pilot Program Rollout**

    - **Activity:** Select one institution—e.g., scholarship fund, training center—and launch a 30-day pilot. Engage at least 20 participants, implement the curriculum, and gather quantitative/qualitative data (surveys, testimonials, performance metrics).

    - **Deliverable:** A "Pilot Impact Report" with insights, outcomes, and action items for scaling.

3. **Day 106–110: Governance Test and Feedback Loop**

    - **Activity:** Convene the Legacy Council to review pilot outcomes; evaluate institutional health against KPIs; refine governance processes based on real-world feedback.

    - **Deliverable:** Revised "Governance & Strategy Update" with adjusted charters, updated KPI targets, and redefined roles as necessary.

4. **Day 111–115: Mentorship Program Kickoff**

    - **Activity:** Launch the first module of the "Legacy Curriculum 101" with mentor-mentee dyads; track progress through milestone assessments; establish a peer cohort of first-line stewards.
    - **Deliverable:** A "Mentorship Program Dashboard" capturing engagement metrics, learning outcomes, and initial feedback.

5. **Day 116–118: Legacy Impact Public Report**

    - **Activity:** Compile a transparent "Legacy Impact Report"—quantify scholarship recipients, training participants, community metrics; include anecdotal success stories and testimonials. Distribute to stakeholders, post on public channels, and archive in the digital repository.
    - **Deliverable:** A 50-page "Legacy Impact Report" PDF and executive summary.

6. **Day 119–120: Future Roadmap and Celebration**

    - **Activity:** Host a "Legacy Constellation Summit" where all stakeholders—Council members, mentors, pilot participants—collaboratively draft your 1-, 3-, and 5-year legacy roadmaps. Conclude with a ceremonial tradition—lighting a beacon or planting a tree—to symbolize growth and continuity.
    - **Deliverable:** A finalized "Legacy Roadmap" document and a commemorative artifact (e.g., inscribed tree planting location coordinates, time capsule contents).

Completion of this **120-Day Legacy Architect Protocol** equips you not only with functioning institutions and programs but also with durable cultural infrastructures and measurement systems. You emerge not just as a strategist but as **an empowered steward** of a legacy that honors those who came before and empowers those who follow.

16.10 Chapter Summary and Forward Look

Purpose and legacy represent the pinnacle of *Cobra Tate* philosophy—transcending personal accomplishments to build enduring frameworks that uplift families, communities, and societies across generations. By articulating your core why, codifying values, constructing legacy institutions, embedding rituals, and executing with rigor, you convert ephemeral success into **living legacies**.

As you conclude this chapter, reflect: What will your epitaph read? How will the world remember your contributions? Remember Tristan Tate's admonition: *"Accomplishment honours your ancestors."*

The journey does not end here—it merely ascends to grander scales. In your subsequent endeavors—whether philanthropic, entrepreneurial, or familial—carry this legacy blueprint as both compass and covenant. Live as if every choice echoes across time, and let your legacy be the answer not only to personal ambition but to the silent calls of generations untold.

A new dawn of purpose awaits: step forward, architect of legacy, and shape the world that future ages will celebrate.

> "He who masters his emotions masters the world."
> — **Tristan Tate**

Chapter 17: Emotional Mastery — The Stoic Warrior Within

Emotions are the currents beneath the surface of every decision, every action, and every relationship. In the *Cobra Tate* universe, **emotional mastery** is not about suppressing feeling but rather cultivating a disciplined interplay between reason and passion—where raw energy is harnessed, channeled, and transformed into unwavering purpose. This chapter unpacks the exhaustive roadmap to becoming a Stoic warrior of emotion: from the origins of Tate's emotional doctrine to the psychological architectures that underpin self-regulation; from the four pillars of emotional resilience to daily and weekly rituals; from advanced frameworks for real-time emotion calibration to case studies showcasing transformative breakthroughs; from common derailments to corrective strategies; from philosophical bedrocks of stoicism and modern neuroscience to a rigorous 120-day "Emotional Warrior" protocol. By immersing in this paradigm, you will convert reactive impulses into strategic opportunities, ensuring that your emotional state becomes an ally rather than an adversary in your quest for greatness.

17.1 The Nature and Necessity of Emotional Mastery

Emotional mastery is the art and science of understanding, directing, and adapting one's affective states to align with long-term objectives. Emotional intelligence (EQ) frameworks typically focus on self-awareness, self-regulation, social awareness, and relationship management. *Cobra Tate* extends this into a combative synthesis—emotions as both weapons and shields in life's battles. Key imperatives include:

1. **Emotion as Energy**

    - **Raw Power:** Emotions, when understood and harnessed, provide bursts of motivation, clarity, and connection that pure logic cannot deliver.

    - **Directing Energy:** Just as an athlete channels adrenaline into performance, the Stoic warrior channels anger into focus, anxiety into preparation, and joy into sustained momentum.

2. **Emotion as Information**

    - **Signal Interpretation:** Emotions signal underlying values, unmet needs, and potential threats. For instance, persistent frustration often indicates misalignment between goals and actions—an invitation to recalibrate strategy.

    - **Cognitive Feedback Loop:** By attending to emotional data (e.g., noticing rising irritation during negotiation), the disciplined mind can execute a cognitive hack—pausing, reframing, and choosing a measured response.

3. **Emotion as Influence**

    - **Interpersonal Dynamics:** Mastery over one's emotional tone shapes how others respond—confidence, calm, and empathy engender trust, leadership, and magnetism.

    - **Social Leverage:** A controlled emotional presence can defuse conflict, galvanize teams, and shape cultural climates—essential for legacy architects and empire builders alike.

Without emotional mastery, one becomes a hostage to instinctual reactivity—responding reflexively rather than strategically. With mastery, emotions transform from unpredictable liabilities into **reliable assets** that augment any pursuit.

17.2 Origins of Tate's Emotional Doctrine

17.2.1 Early Trials in the Ring

- **First Gloves:** At age ten, Andrew's initial sparring sessions produced tears as frequently as triumphs. Early bouts revealed that technical skill meant little if fear, frustration, or elation dictated his actions. Through repeated knockdowns—each a crucible event—Andrew learned that **composure under duress** is the true measure of a champion.

- **Controlled Aggression:** He discovered that raw aggression without restraint led to overcommitment and vulnerability. Instead, channeling the "fight-or-flight" surge into standardized combination drills, he cultivated a measured ferocity—**aggression steered by intent** rather than impulse.

17.2.2 Business Betrayals and Emotional Leverage

- **Webcam Empire Collapse:** In 2017, when the Dominion of Malta froze accounts and deplatformed Andrew's primary revenue streams, initial anger threatened rash retaliation. Instead, he used that emotional fire to fuel strategic pivots: rebuilding on Bitcoin-friendly platforms and constructing a more decentralized revenue architecture.

- **Digital Deplatforming:** Experiencing successive bans on YouTube and Facebook sharpened his understanding that **resentment and despair** are wasted calories. By applying Emotional Reframing—identifying deplatforming as a catalyst for digital sovereignty—he maintained composure and harnessed indignation into **relentless self-proliferation** on alternative networks.

17.2.3 Familial Loss and the Stoic Imperative

- **Father's Battle with Cancer:** When Emory Tate's health declined, Andrew and Tristan witnessed firsthand how grief and helplessness can cripple even the strongest wills. By practicing deliberate Emotional Distancing—acknowledging sorrow without succumbing—they remained present, providing support without panicking. Emory's passing crystallized their Stoic resolve: **pain is inevitable; suffering is optional**.

These crucibles formed the bedrock of Tate's emotional doctrine: an unblinking gaze into adversity, willed detachment when necessary, and the relentless repurposing of emotional upheaval into **strategic advantage**.

17.3 The Four Pillars of Emotional Resilience

To structure emotional mastery, Tate prescribes four interlocking pillars—each a domain requiring dedicated cultivation:

Pillar 1: Self-Awareness and Emotional Literacy

- **Emotion Identification:** Develop a granular vocabulary for emotional states (e.g., distinguishing frustration from indignation, anxiety from adrenaline). Use constructs such as Plutchik's Wheel of Emotions to map primary (joy, sadness, anger, fear, surprise, disgust, trust, anticipation) and secondary emotions (e.g., hostility, vigilance, admiration).

- **Physiological Awareness:** Learn to detect somatic signals—heart rate, muscle tension, breathing patterns—that correlate with specific emotions. For instance, a tightening in the chest often signals emerging rage; a hollow sensation in the gut may prelude anxiety.

- **Cognitive Labeling:** Utilize techniques like "Name It to Tame It": when you feel an emotional surge, pause, and mentally label it—"This is irritation" or "This is excitement." Labeling engages the prefrontal cortex, diminishing amygdala hijack.

Pillar 2: Self-Regulation and Impulse Control

- **Cognitive Reappraisal:** Reframe emotionally charged stimuli. If a negotiation becomes heated, reappraise the counterpart's hostility as "strategic posturing" rather than personal attack, thereby deflating anger and re-centering on tactical objectives.

- **Delay and Distance (The 10-Second Rule):** Institute a habitual pause—a minimum 10-second mental count—before reacting to provocation. During this window, practice deep diaphragmatic breathing to engage the parasympathetic response and prevent impulsive escalation.

- **Emotional Scripting:** Pre-write "if–then" plans for high-stakes scenarios: "If I receive a hostile message, then I will respond with a calm, fact-based clarification." These scripts, repeated and internalized, become autopilot responses under stress.

Pillar 3: Emotional Transformation and Channeling

- **Adversity Alchemy:** Convert negative emotions (fear, anger, grief) into productive energy. For instance, transform fear of failure into "fear-fueled preparation"—draft multiple plans, simulate potential failure modes, and rehearse contingencies.

- **Positive Intensification:** Amplify constructive emotions—confidence, gratitude, passion—to saturate mental states. Use techniques such as "Victory Visualizations" (detailed mental rehearsal of past triumphs) to rekindle confidence before critical engagements.

- **Kinesthetic Anchoring:** Pair specific physical actions (clenching fists, adopting power stances, tapping a rune-like pattern) with desired emotional states. Through consistent repetition, these anchors trigger emotional shifts on command (akin to Pavlovian conditioning, as popularized by Tony Robbins's "anchoring" concept).

Pillar 4: Emotional Resilience Under Fire

- **Stress Exposure Training:** Integrate controlled stressors—cold plunges, high-intensity interval training, simulated public speaking—into weekly routines to condition emotional equilibrium under duress. Each exposure session should incrementally increase intensity to expand one's tolerance envelope.

- **Stoic Endurance Practices:** Emulate the Stoic exercise of "premeditatio malorum"—regularly visualize worst-case scenarios (financial loss, public humiliation, physical injury) and plan psychological responses. By pre-experiencing adversity mentally, actual occurrences trigger less shock and a faster recovery.

- **Recovery and Restoration:** Employ active recovery rituals—cold therapy, breathwork, journaling—to dissipate accumulated emotional tolls. Recognize that resilience is not limitless; scheduled decompression (digital detox, nature immersion, creative expression) is necessary to replenish emotional bandwidth.

Mastering these pillars transforms the emotional landscape from a wild frontier into a controlled arena where you command states rather than being commanded by them.

17.4 Daily and Weekly Emotional Mastery Rituals

Consistency is the forge in which emotional resilience is welded. Integrate these daily and weekly rituals into your regimen:

17.4.1 Morning Emotional Calibration (Daily, 5:15 AM – 5:45 AM)

- **Emotion Check-In (5 minutes):** Upon waking, place one hand on your chest and one on your abdomen; close your eyes and scan for residual emotional residues—residual anxiety, excitement, or lingering tension from dreams. Label each emotion succinctly (e.g., "I feel a flicker of anxiety"), note it in your digital journal, then release it with an exhalation.

- **Stoic Journaling (10 minutes):** Respond to the prompt: "What challenges might I face today, and how will I respond virtuously?" Write at least one scenario (e.g., "A colleague may challenge my authority; I will respond with calm questions rather than defensiveness."). This prepares your mind to anticipate emotional triggers.

- **Power Pose Activation (5 minutes):** Engage in a series of power poses—feet shoulder-width apart, hands on hips, chin slightly raised—for two minutes, while repeating an affirmation (e.g., "I am calm, focused, and unshakable"). Follow with two minutes of controlled diaphragmatic breathing (inhale for 4, hold for 2, exhale for 6) to link physical posture with emotional calm.

17.4.2 Midday Equilibrium Check (Daily, 12:00 PM – 12:15 PM)

- **Physiological Scan (3 minutes):** Briefly close your eyes, scan body from head to toe—notice tension in shoulders, neck, jaw, or stomach. If tension is detected, perform gentle neck rolls, shoulder shrugs, and a seated spinal twist for relief.

- **Micro-Meditation (7 minutes):** Using a guided app or timer, practice focused-attention meditation—focus solely on the breath entering and exiting the nostrils. When the mind wanders, gently return to the breath without judgment. This resets cognitive load and regulates mid-day stress.

- **Emotion Labeling and Reframing (5 minutes):** Write in your journal: "Current emotional state: ____." Then ask yourself: "What thought or scenario triggered this? How can I reinterpret it to serve my objectives?" For example, if frustration emerges due to email backlog, reframe as "This backlog signals high demand—an opportunity to delegate or automate."

17.4.3 Evening Emotional Debrief (Daily, 8:30 PM – 9:00 PM)

- **Triadic Reflection (10 minutes):** In your journal, answer three questions:

    1. "What emotion dominated my day?" (e.g., impatience)

    2. "What triggered it?" (e.g., waiting for delayed deliverables)

    3. "How did I respond, and how could I have responded more skillfully?" (e.g., I responded by brooding; next time, I will send a status update and use the waiting time for productive solo work.)

- **Gratitude & Release (5 minutes):** List three positive experiences that elicited joy, pride, or peace—no matter how small (e.g., a productive call, a supportive colleague, a brisk evening walk). Conclude each with the phrase "I accept and release all other emotions that no longer serve me."

- **Sleep Hygiene Wind-Down (5 minutes):** Perform a short guided Progressive Muscle Relaxation (PMR) exercise—tensing and relaxing each muscle group from toes to forehead—while visualizing stress melting away. This makes the transition to restorative sleep smoother, ensuring emotional resilience replenishment.

17.4.4 Weekly "Emotion Fireside" (Weekly, Sunday Evening, 2 Hours)

- **Emotional Metrics Review (30 minutes):** Review your daily journal entries, categorize emotional highs/lows on a simple spreadsheet (e.g., rating intensity 1–10, noting context). Calculate the frequency of specific triggers (e.g., 5 instances of frustration related to communication).

- **Group Vulnerability Circle (45 minutes):** Convene a small, trusted cohort (3–5 members) for a "Vulnerability Circle": each shares one emotional challenge from the week, the underlying cause, and one strategy they plan to employ. Peers offer constructive feedback, empathetic listening, and ritualistic encouragement (e.g., a solidarity fist bump or brief affirmation).

- **Stoic Text Study (30 minutes):** Read a passage from Stoic classics—Marcus Aurelius's *Meditations*, Seneca's Letters, or Epictetus's Enchiridion—focusing on emotional themes. Discuss how these ancient insights apply to modern stressors (e.g., social media outrage, financial volatility).

- **Ritualistic Reaffirmation (15 minutes):** Conclude with a symbolic ritual: light a single candle to represent "clarity of mind," state your emotional commitment for the week ahead (e.g., "I commit to transforming anxiety into strategic preparation"), and extinguish the flame—symbolizing release of past emotional burdens.

By institutionalizing these rituals, emotional mastery ceases to be sporadic and instead becomes a **non-negotiable pillar** of your daily routine.

17.5 Advanced Frameworks for Real-Time Emotion Calibration

To elevate from routine regulation to real-time calibration—responding to unfolding scenarios with precision—adopt these advanced methodologies:

17.5.1 The "S.T.O.P." Framework

An immediate intervention executed in four steps:

1. **Stop (S):** When an emotional surge occurs—irritation, panic, triumph—verbally or mentally utter "Stop." This interrupts automatic reactivity.

2. **Take a Breath (T):** Inhale slowly for 4 counts, hold for 2, exhale for 6—recruiting the parasympathetic nervous system to downregulate intensity.

3. **Observe (O):** Without judgment, identify:

   - **Emotion:** What am I feeling?

   - **Trigger:** What event, thought, or memory sparked this?

   - **Beneath the Emotion:** Is there a core value or need (safety, respect, autonomy) at risk?

4. **Proceed (P):** Choose the most appropriate response aligned with your objectives. If rage threatened to derail a negotiation, you might respond with a factual question: "Can you clarify why you believe that point?" rather than a heated retort.

The S.T.O.P. framework, practiced until reflexive, becomes **instinctual armor** against emotional hijack.

17.5.2 The "C.A.L.M." Protocol for High-Stakes Moments

For situations where emotional stakes run highest—public speaking, boardroom debates, crisis management—employ the "C.A.L.M." protocol:

1. **Center (C):** Physically ground yourself—plant feet firmly on the floor, roll shoulders back, center weight midline. This posture primes you for composure.

2. **Acknowledge (A):** Internally acknowledge the presence of intensity—"I am aware of my racing heart and tight chest." Externalize if appropriate—"I want you to know I am fully present."

3. **Label (L):** Mentally label the primary emotion—"This is frustration." Labeling shifts processing from the amygdala to the prefrontal cortex, diminishing reactivity.

4. **Moderate (M):** Choose a micro-behavior to modulate intensity—take a brief sip of water, adjust your eyeglasses, or reposition your feet—engaging sensorimotor pathways that reduce emotional arousal.

Using C.A.L.M. in high-stakes scenarios preserves mental acuity and ensures that **presence and clarity** prevail over panic or reflexive passion.

17.5.3 The "Emotional Vantage Point" Exercise

An advanced mental simulation that fosters perspective and long-term equanimity:

1. **Time Travel Visualization:** Imagine observing your current emotional state from a vantage point 10 years in the future—ask: "In 2034, when I think back to this moment of anger/anxiety/excitement, how significant will it seem? Will the cause matter?"

2. **Narrative Reframing:** Craft a brief future-retrospective narrative: "Looking back, I see how this challenge was a necessary step toward resilience; I appreciate that I responded with courage."

3. **Contextual Integration:** Use insights from this simulation to temper present reactions—if you recognize that the trigger is likely ephemeral, you can respond with measured composure rather than magnified agitation.

This practice cultivates **temporal temperance**, reducing the gravitational pull of immediate emotional turbulence.

17.6 Case Studies: Transformative Emotional Mastery

17.6.1 The Negotiator Who Turned Rage into Resolution

A high-stakes corporate negotiator faced a counterpart who repeatedly attempted to bait him into rage:

- **Initial Reaction:** In early sessions, he exploded—yelling at the table—derailing deals and damaging credibility.

- **Technique Adoption:** After adopting the S.T.O.P. framework, he began labeling sudden irritation ("This is manipulation"), taking controlled breaths, and responding with calm, fact-based inquiries ("What data supports that claim?").

- **Outcome:** Over three months, his negotiation win rate rose from 55% to 83%. The counterpart, unable to provoke him, conceded more favorable terms. Moreover, several observers noted his calm presence and requested his mentorship, expanding his internal network.

17.6.2 The Athlete Who Overcame Performance Anxiety

An elite kickboxer, preparing for a world title bout, suffered debilitating pre-fight anxiety—vomiting, sleepless nights, and panic attacks:

- **Initial Intervention:** Began S.T.O.P. practice three weeks before the fight—each time anxiety spiked (during walking through hotel corridors, moments before weigh-ins), he paused, breathed, observed physical sensations, and reminded himself of past victories.

- **Real-Time Calibration:** In the dressing room, deployed C.A.L.M.—centering stance, labeling adrenaline as "focus," and moderating by applying a pressure-point massage to his temples to diffuse tension.

- **Result:** He entered the ring with palpable calm; during the bout, even after being knocked down in the second round, he maintained composure, came back to execute a fight-ending combination, and won by knockout. Post-fight interviews revealed that emotional mastery, not technical superiority, was the decisive factor.

17.6.3 The CEO Who Led Her Company Through Crisis

A tech startup CEO faced a sudden data breach and ensuing customer outrage—up to 50% of subscriptions canceled within 48 hours:

- **Emotional Spiral:** Initial panic threatened to derail her clarity; she felt guilt, shame, and fear that her leadership would collapse.

- **Ritual Invocation:** She retreated to her office, performed a brief Stoic Journaling exercise—"What is within my control? What is not? How will I respond virtuously?"—then instituted a C.A.L.M. approach during her next all-hands address: centered posture, acknowledged collective pain, labeled systemic failure (not personal inadequacy), and moderated by announcing a clear remediation roadmap.

- **Outcome:** Her composed response rallied the team; transparency and decisive action—patching the breach, offering free six-month extensions—reversed cancellations. Six months later, revenue soared 150% above pre-crisis levels, and employee retention hit an all-time high. The board lauded her "unshakeable calm under fire" as exemplary leadership.

17.7 Pitfalls and Corrections: Emotional Mastery Saboteurs

Even the most disciplined can stumble. Common pitfalls include:

1. **Emotional Suppression**

    - **Symptom:** Habitually pushing down feelings, leading to sudden, disproportionate outbursts or psychosomatic ailments (e.g., ulcers, insomnia).
    - **Correction:** Adopt "Willingness to Feel"—a practice of allowing emotions to surface, journaling about them without filtering, and sharing with a trusted ally or therapist. Integrate weekly "Safe Release Sessions" where, within privacy, you express pent-up emotions through writing, art, or physical exertion (e.g., weighted punching bag sessions).

2. **Over-Identification with Emotions**

    - **Symptom:** Belief that "I am my anger" or "I am my fear," leading to confirmation biases and self-fulfilling prophecies.
    - **Correction:** Reinforce "Observer Self" through mindfulness. Regularly practice "Witness Exercises": imagine your emotions as passing clouds or fleeting waves—recognize them but do not equate them with your identity. Use guided meditations focusing on the "narrator" perspective to strengthen this distinction.

3. **Emotionally Contagious Environments**

    - **Symptom:** Being swept up by collective emotional waves—group panic during market crashes, mob mentality in social media outrage.
    - **Correction:** Construct "Emotionally Shielded Spaces" by maintaining private emotional calibration rituals and limiting exposure to sensationalist group dynamics. If a team meeting descends into chaos, pause proceedings, enact a two-minute silent reflection, and resume with composed agendas.

4. **Chronic Hypervigilance**

    - **Symptom:** Constant scanning for threats—personal, financial, reputational—resulting in sustained cortisol elevation, sleep disruption, and decision fatigue.

- **Correction:** Utilize "Safety Scripts": anchor statements reinforcing security ("I am prepared; I have contingencies; I trust my judgment"). Combine with scheduled "Relaxed Awareness" windows—periods deliberately spent in low-stimulation activities (e.g., reading philosophy, gardening, gentle yoga) to retrain baseline arousal levels downward.

5. **Misplaced Emotional Alchemy**

    - **Symptom:** Channeling emotional energy into destructive or misaligned activities—e.g., channeling grief into reckless risk-taking, fueling anger into unproductive conflicts.

    - **Correction:** Develop "Value Alignment Checks": before directing emotional energy, ask, "Does this action advance my ultimate mission and honor my values?" If not, redirect to a neutral vessel—physical exercise, creative outlet, or strategic planning rather than retaliatory confrontation.

By diagnosing these saboteurs and implementing corrective levers, you maintain **a balanced emotional ecosystem**, where energy flows optimally toward purposeful outcomes.

17.8 Philosophical Foundations: Stoicism, Neuroscience, and Modern Psychology

Emotional mastery in the *Cobra Tate* model synthesizes ancient wisdom with cutting-edge science:

17.8.1 Stoicism: The Foundation of Equanimity

- **Epictetus's Dichotomy of Control:** Recognize that external events lie beyond your direct influence; only your judgments, choices, and efforts are within control.

- **Marcus Aurelius's Meditations on Impermanence:** Reflecting that every hardship and triumph is transient reduces attachment to outcomes, enabling serenity under shifting circumstances.

- **Seneca's On Anger:** Illustrates that unbridled wrath corrupts reason; the antidote lies in swift recognition and deliberate reorientation.

Stoicism equips the warrior with **cognitive scaffolding** to interpret events dispassionately and act virtuously, regardless of emotional currents.

17.8.2 Modern Neuroscience: The Mechanics of Emotion

- **Amygdala Hijack and Prefrontal Regulation:** Emotional storms originate in the amygdala's rapid threat detection; the prefrontal cortex's regulation is delayed. Techniques such as labeling, breathing, and mindful attention shift neural activity from limbic regions to executive networks, restoring rational deliberation.

- **Neuroplasticity and Habit Formation:** Consistent emotional regulation exercises (e.g., daily journaling, S.T.O.P. usage) physically rewire synapses—strengthening prefrontal control circuits and dampening hyperactive emotional responses.

- **Polyvagal Theory:** Understanding the autonomic nervous system's ventral vagal complex (social engagement), sympathetic (fight-or-flight), and dorsal vagal (shutdown) branches allows strategic engagement of **social co-regulation**—seeking positive human connection during distress to activate the ventral vagal state and promote calm.

17.8.3 Contemporary Psychology: Integrative Approaches

- **Cognitive Behavioral Therapy (CBT):** Highlights how distorted cognitions (e.g., catastrophizing, black-and-white thinking) fuel maladaptive emotions. The practice of disputing irrational beliefs dovetails with Tate's Cognitive Reappraisal techniques.

- **Dialectical Behavior Therapy (DBT):** Emphasizes balancing acceptance and change—validating emotions while striving to modify them. DBT's "Opposite Action" (acting contrary to the emotion-driven urge) parallels Tate's emphasis on channeling negative feeling into productive activity (e.g., using anger to fuel a training session).

- **Emotional Awareness and Expression Therapy (EAET):** Encourages open expression of core emotions, especially trauma-related, to relieve chronic stress. Tate's "Safe Release Sessions" echo EAET by providing structured opportunities to externalize and transform deep-seated feelings.

By weaving Stoic virtue ethics, neuroscientific insight, and modern therapeutic modalities, *Cobra Tate* crafts an emotional mastery paradigm that is both **timeless** and **empirically grounded**.

17.9 Your 120-Day "Emotional Warrior" Protocol

To forge unbreakable emotional resilience and mastery, undertake this comprehensive **120-day protocol**, divided into four 30-day stages:

Stage 1: Foundation of Emotional Literacy (Days 1–30)

1. **Day 1–3: Baseline Assessment**

   - **Self-Reporting:** Complete a validated Emotional Intelligence assessment (e.g., EQ-i 2.0 or MSCEIT) to gauge strengths and gaps across self-awareness, self-regulation, empathy, and social skills.

   - **Situational Audit:** List the five most frequent emotional triggers in your life (e.g., deadline pressure, interpersonal conflict, financial uncertainty).

   - **Somatic Recall:** Record three incidents from the past week where physical sensations (tight chest, racing heart) corralled your emotional state.

2. **Day 4–10: Emotion Identification Drills**

   - **Emotion Wheel Practice:** Each morning, select one hour's span to note every discrete emotion experienced, mapping it onto Plutchik's Wheel categories; aim for at least 50 unique labels by Day 10 (e.g., annoyance, indignation, exasperation, frustration).

   - **Daily "Name It" Meditation:** Spend 5 minutes post-lunch meditating and silently labeling any dominant emotion present without judgment. Log observations.

3. **Day 11–20: Physiological Awareness and Labeling**

   - **Somatic Mapping Journal:** Each evening, for at least one emotional event, note the precise physical cues (heart rate measured by a wearable, muscle tension reported subjectively, breath pattern) and the corresponding emotion.

   - **Breath-Labeled Interventions:** Upon noticing an emotional trigger, practice the "Label and Breathe" technique—name the emotion, take three measured diaphragmatic breaths, and note changes in sensation. Aim for four such interventions daily.

4. **Day 21–30: Emotional Scripting and Micro-Response Plans**

   - **Identify Top Three Triggers:** Rank the five triggers by frequency or intensity; select the top three to script "if–then" response plans (e.g., "If I feel imposter syndrome before a presentation, then I will recite three validated achievements and take a one-minute grounding breath").

   - **Rehearsal Ritual:** Each day, enact one scripted plan in a low-stakes scenario or through visualization, reinforcing neural pathways for future real-world application.

Stage 2: Building Self-Regulation and Impulse Control (Days 31–60)

1. **Day 31–35: S.T.O.P. Framework Conditioning**

    - **Daily "Micro-S.T.O.P." Sessions:** At least five times daily, intentionally pause mid-action (e.g., while walking, during a conversation) to perform the S.T.O.P. sequence—speak "Stop," breathe, observe, proceed. Log each instance and note any reduction in spontaneous reactivity.

    - **Accountability Partner Check:** Pair with a trusted peer; each evening, text one another "S.T.O.P. successes"—briefly describe when you used the framework and the outcome.

2. **Day 36–45: C.A.L.M. Protocol Mastery**

    - **Guided Exposure:** Use audio-visual cues (e.g., recorded arguments, high-intensity sports clips, provocative statements) to intentionally trigger moderate emotional responses. Practice C.A.L.M. in response—center, acknowledge, label, moderate—until each step becomes automatic.

    - **Real-Life Application:** Identify at least three real-world high-stakes moments (e.g., team meetings, sensitive emails) and apply C.A.L.M. Schedule these events during the day and debrief outcomes each evening.

3. **Day 46–55: Kinesthetic Anchoring Techniques**

    - **Anchor Identification:** Choose two distinct physical anchors—one for "focused calm" (e.g., pressing thumb and middle finger together) and one for "motivational arousal" (e.g., clenching fists at sides). Pair each anchor with a positive emotion during controlled practice—visualize calm, press anchor, hold for five seconds; visualize energy, perform motivational anchor.

    - **Daily Anchor Drills:** Perform each anchor-drill cycle (visualization plus anchor) five times throughout the day—upon waking, mid-morning, post-lunch, mid-afternoon, before bed—reinforcing the anchor's neural association.

4. **Day 56–60: Stoic Endurance Practices**

- **Premeditatio Malorum Sessions:** Each morning, spend 10 minutes writing three "worst-case scenarios" for the day (e.g., project failure, criticism, personal conflict) and script verdict-based responses grounded in core values.
- **Controlled Stressor Exposure:** Schedule one daily stressor—cold plunge bath (minimum 45 seconds), high-intensity interval workout, or a brief public speaking challenge—followed by a debrief noting emotional responses and chosen stoic reframes (e.g., "I embraced the shock of cold as training for adversity in business").

Stage 3: Emotional Transformation and Real-Time Calibration (Days 61–90)

1. **Day 61–65: Adversity Alchemy Protocol**

    - **Mapping Negative Emotions to Objectives:** Create a table listing five recent negative emotions (e.g., jealousy, self-doubt, despair). For each, assign a corresponding productive channel (e.g., jealousy → study competitor strategies; self-doubt → compile a wins list; despair → schedule community service).
    - **Action Execution:** Over the next five days, commit to executing at least one channeling activity per emotion within two hours of recognizing it. Journal outcomes and sense of control.

2. **Day 66–75: Positive Intensification Techniques**

    - **Victory Visualization Library:** Curate a collection of 10–15 short (1–2 minute) mental rehearsals of past accomplishments—writing them as vivid narratives. Each day, select two visualizations: one in the morning (to energize) and one mid-afternoon (to recalibrate).
    - **Gratitude Amplification:** Each evening, not only list three things you're grateful for, but also elaborate on why each is significant—explaining how each has materially or emotionally shaped you.

3. **Day 76–85: Emotional Vantage Point Drills**

    - **Future Self Journaling:** Twice weekly, write a 500-word letter from your future self (five years hence) back to present you—discussing present emotional challenges and advising on maintaining perspective (e.g., "You will laugh at how anxious you were about that missed deal").

- **Perspective Sessions:** During moments of high stress, immediately pause, recite: "In ten years, will I care about this? Will this matter to my grandkids?" and journal one sentence on resulting shifts in intensity.

4. **Day 86–90: Integration of C.A.L.M. and S.T.O.P. into Flow States**

    - **Flow-State Initiation Rituals:** Identify tasks where you want to achieve flow (e.g., creative writing, complex coding). Before starting, perform C.A.L.M.—center posture, acknowledge potential distractions, label them, moderate to clarity—then use S.T.O.P. at the first sign of drift.

    - **Flow Metrics:** Record time to entry into flow (how many minutes before deep focus), duration of uninterrupted flow, and subjective flow quality (on a 1–10 scale). Aim to decrease time to flow by 20% each week and increase duration by 15%.

Stage 4: Emotional Resilience Under Fire and Long-Term Stewardship (Days 91–120)

1. **Day 91–95: High-Stakes Simulation Mastery**

    - **Scenario Design:** Collaborate with a peer to craft five realistic, high-emotion crisis simulations relevant to your domain (e.g., product recall announcement, public speaking under heckling, abrupt leadership restructuring). Role-play each scenario twice—once unannounced to capture raw reaction, once with full C.A.L.M./S.T.O.P. deployment.

    - **Performance Debrief:** After each session, analyze response latency, emotional intensity (self-rated 1–10), and strategic outcome. Document corrective adjustments for next iteration.

2. **Day 96–105: Community Co-Regulation and Social Calibration**

    - **Group Emotional Resilience Workshops:** Host a two-day workshop for 10–15 participants, teaching S.T.O.P., C.A.L.M., and anchoring techniques. Include live drills—rapid-fire provocations where trainees must apply frameworks to maintain composure.

- **Co-Regulation Pods:** Form ongoing peer pods (3–4 members each) tasked with weekly emotional sharing circles. Each pod assigns one member per week to share a personal emotional struggle; peers provide guided feedback using Socratic questioning—ensuring collective growth and reinforcing community bonds.

3. **Day 106–115: Legacy Emotion Transmission**

    - **Intergenerational Emotion Dialogues:** Invite older and younger generations (family members, mentees) to share emotional challenge stories—focusing on how they overcame adversity. Structure dialogues with guiding questions:

        1. "What was the pivotal moment of emotional overwhelm?"
        2. "Which techniques did you use to reclaim control?"
        3. "How has that experience shaped your approach to subsequent challenges?"

    - **Emotion Archive Compilation:** Record and transcribe dialogues, extract key emotional lessons, and compile into a rudimentary "Family Emotional Manual" or "Organization Emotional Playbook." This resource preserves emotional wisdom for future generations.

4. **Day 116–120: Reflection, Consolidation, and Future Roadmap**

    - **Comprehensive Emotional Audit:** Re-administer the EQ assessment used in Stage 1; compare pre- and post-protocol scores across self-awareness, regulation, motivation, empathy, and social skills.

    - **Success Narrative:** Write a 1,500-word reflective essay chronicling your 120-day transformation—highlighting key turning points, paradigm shifts, and emotional breakthroughs.

    - **Long-Term Emotional Stewardship Plan:** Draft a "Lifetime Emotional Mastery Roadmap," outlining periodic practices (e.g., quarterly Stoic text study, monthly emotional journaling retreats, annual high-stakes simulations) to maintain and deepen emotional resilience. Identify future emotional growth areas (e.g., deepening empathy, refining conflict resolution) and resource commitments.

Completion of this **120-Day Emotional Warrior Protocol** ensures you have not only mastered immediate emotional regulation but also instituted a perpetually adaptive system—guaranteeing that your emotional state remains **a strategic ally** no matter the circumstances.

17.10 Chapter Summary and Forward Look

Emotional mastery is the crucible in which the Stoic warrior temper his spirit—transmuting tumult into tranquility, fury into focus, and vulnerability into valor. Through an unwavering commitment to emotional literacy, rigorous self-regulation, transformative channeling, and resilience training, you establish an inner citadel from which no external storm can dislodge you. By integrating ancient Stoic wisdom with modern neuroscientific techniques and psychological insights, *Cobra Tate* forges a paradigm of emotional sovereignty—essential for navigating the complexities of leadership, entrepreneurship, relationships, and legacy.

As you complete this chapter's exhaustive protocols and rituals, remember Tristan Tate's charge: *"He who masters his emotions masters the world."*

Ahead lies Chapter 18: **Physical Vitality and Longevity**—a comprehensive treatise on extending not only the breadth of your influence but the duration of your presence on this earth. Prepare to fortify body and spirit in unison, ensuring that your emotional mastery is matched by an indomitable physical vessel capable of sustaining an extraordinary life.

Forge onward: with emotions as your ally, every battle—personal or professional—becomes an opportunity for greater triumph.

> "Your body is the vessel of your ambition; preserve it as you would your kingdom."
> — **Tristan Tate**

Chapter 18: Physical Vitality and Longevity — The Eternal Engine

Physical vitality is the unspoken cornerstone of every triumph. In the *Cobra Tate* canon, strength of body begets clarity of mind; endurance of spirit; and resilience of will. Yet, beyond mere athletic prowess lies a deeper objective: **to extend your healthspan alongside your lifespan**, ensuring that every victory—from personal conquests to generational legacies—unfolds with the vigor you deserve. This chapter delivers an exhaustive master-plan for cultivating lifelong vitality and longevity: tracing Tate's own evolution, defining the four foundational pillars, prescribing rigorous daily and weekly rituals, unveiling advanced frameworks (from periodization to biohacking), illustrating transformative case studies, diagnosing common pitfalls with precise remedies, grounding the approach in ancient and modern wisdom, and guiding you through a 120-day "Vitality Architect" protocol designed to forge the indomitable physical vessel requisite for a legend in the making.

18.1 The Vital Link Between Body and Purpose

Every ounce of mental fortitude and strategic insight demands a robust physical chassis. Without vitality:

- **Mental Acuity Fades** — chronic fatigue and poor metabolic health erode focus, memory, and creativity.

- **Emotional Resilience Wanes** — hormonal imbalances, inflammation, and sleep deficits amplify stress reactivity.

- **Purpose Is Imperiled** — no empire, no legacy can be built upon a body riddled with preventable decline.

Conversely, a thriving physiology delivers:

1. **Peak Cognitive Performance** — optimized nutrient flow and neurotrophic support sharpen decision velocity.

2. **Sustained Energy** — metabolic flexibility allows effortless shifts between fuel sources, eliminating energy slumps.

3. **Enhanced Recovery** — cellular repair mechanisms, when primed, neutralize damage and rebuild stronger tissue.

In *Cobra Tate* philosophy, your body is **both your primary investment and your primary return**—nurture it, and every other domain of excellence flourishes.

18.2 Origins of Tate's Vitality Ethos

18.2.1 Combat Forged Resilience

- **Early Regimen:** At 15, Andrew's routine included 10 km dawn runs, midday sparring, and evening strength circuits—often totaling six training hours per day. He quickly learned that **consistency, not volume alone**, cemented progress.

- **Injury and Adaptation:** A torn pectoral muscle threatened to end his kickboxing career. Forced to pause, he pivoted to mobility drills and isometric holds—discovering that **joint integrity and mind-muscle connection** were as vital as raw power.

18.2.2 Entrepreneurial Endurance

- **Traveling the Globe:** Building his casino empire in Eastern Europe involved 18-hour days, jet lag, and high-stress negotiations. Andrew aknowledged that **travel-related sleep debt** and irregular nutrition were his unseen adversaries. He instituted portable meal kits and circadian alignment strategies—lighting protocols and timed supplementation—to preserve performance.

18.2.3 Near-Death Catalyst

- **Medical Emergency:** A severe bout of food poisoning during a multi-day retreat left him bedridden and despondent. This brush with mortality crystallized his conviction that **longevity is not a luxury but a necessity** for the realization of one's grandest ambitions. He began to study gerontology, mitochondrial function, and hormonal optimization—laying the groundwork for a full-spectrum vitality doctrine.

These crucibles shaped Tate's approach: not merely to survive, but to thrive—harnessing adversity as the catalyst for **a lifelong pursuit of physical sovereignty**.

18.3 The Four Pillars of Vitality

To structure your ascent to peak health and extended lifespan, *Cobra Tate* prescribes four interdependent pillars:

Pillar 1: Precision Nutrition

- **Macronutrient Mastery:** Calculate protein (1.2–1.8 g/kg lean mass), fats (0.5–1.0 g/kg emphasizing omega-3 sources), and carbohydrates (timed around activity for glycogen replenishment).

- **Micronutrient Sufficiency:** Regularly assay levels of vitamin D, B12, magnesium, zinc, and antioxidants; tailor supplementation to deficiencies.

- **Chrono-Nutritional Strategies:** Align eating windows with circadian rhythms—typically an 8- to 10-hour feeding window to evoke intermittent fasting benefits for autophagy and metabolic health.

Pillar 2: Structured Training and Movement

- **Resistance Periodization:** Four-week hypertrophy blocks (8–12 reps) followed by four-week strength blocks (3–5 reps), interspersed with power phases focusing on Olympic-style lifts and plyometrics.

- **Aerobic and Anaerobic Balance:** Two interval sessions (sprinting, rowing) paired with one steady-state cardio (60–75% max HR) weekly to optimize cardiovascular health and mitochondrial density.

- **Functional Mobility:** Daily dynamic warm-ups (leg swings, hip circles) and evening static stretching or yoga flows to preserve range of motion and prevent injury.

Pillar 3: Advanced Recovery and Regeneration

- **Sleep Architecture Optimization:** Enforce strict lights-out by 9:30 PM, maintain 7–9 hours of sleep, and use wearable HRV monitoring to adjust training loads according to recovery status.

- **Hormetic Stressors:** Cold plunges (1–3 minutes at 10–12 °C), infrared sauna sessions (20–30 minutes) three times weekly to stimulate mitochondrial biogenesis and heat-shock protein expression.

- **Myofascial and Neural Release:** Weekly deep-tissue massage, foam rolling, and targeted neurodynamic mobilizations to break down adhesions and enhance proprioception.

Pillar 4: Biohacking and Supplementation

- **Targeted Nootropics:** Clinically-validated compounds—creatine monohydrate, omega-3 EPA/DHA, phosphatidylserine—for cognitive resilience and stress buffering.

- **Longevity Agents:** Metformin mimetics (berberine), NAD^+ precursors (nicotinamide riboside), and senolytic protocols (quercetin + dasatinib under supervision) to support cellular repair and delay senescence.

- **Personalized Biofeedback:** Continuous glucose monitoring, pulse oximetry, and sleep trackers to refine nutrition and sleep in real time.

Full mastery of these pillars erects a fortress of vitality—where every meal, movement, and modulation converges to extend both **healthspan and agency**.

18.4 Daily and Weekly Rituals for Lifelong Vitality

Embedding these pillars into your schedule creates **unbreakable momentum**:

18.4.1 Dawn Activation Sequence (Daily, 5:00 AM – 6:00 AM)

1. **Sunlight Exposure (5:00 – 5:05):** 5 minutes of unfiltered morning light to entrain circadian rhythms and boost cortisol awakening response.

2. **Hydration and Electrolytes (5:05 – 5:10):** 500 mL water with added pinch of Himalayan salt and 1 g magnesium citrate to rehydrate and prime neuromuscular function.

3. **Mobility Flow (5:10 – 5:25):** A 15-minute sequence combining joint circles, dynamic lunges, and spinal rolls to awaken the body.

4. **Power Workout (5:25 – 6:00):**
    - **Resistance Lift (20 min):** Compound movement focus (e.g., squat or deadlift) with progressive loading.
    - **Anaerobic Burst (10 min):** Tabata sprint intervals or battle-rope blasts.
    - **Cool-Down Stretch (5 min):** Targeted fascia release with a lacrosse ball on glutes and calves.

18.4.2 Midday Nutrient Timing and Movement (Daily, 12:00 PM – 12:30 PM)

- **Protein-Rich Meal:** 30–40 g of lean protein with fibrous vegetables, consumed mindfully away from screens to optimize postprandial insulin and satiety signals.

- **Micro-Movement Breaks:** Every 10 minutes for 30 seconds, perform bodyweight movements (air squats, hip bridges) to counteract sedentary stress.

18.4.3 Evening Wind-Down Protocol (Daily, 8:30 PM – 9:30 PM)

1. **Low-Carb Snack (8:30 – 8:40):** Casein protein shake or Greek yogurt with a few almonds to support overnight muscle protein synthesis.

2. **Digital Sunset (8:40 – 8:50):** All screens off; if needed, read a printed Stoic text or listen to calming soundscapes.

3. **Breathwork and Stretch (8:50 – 9:10):**
   - **4–7–8 Breathing:** Four-second inhale, seven-second hold, eight-second exhale for three cycles.
   - **Progressive Muscle Relaxation:** Tense and release muscle groups systematically to induce parasympathetic dominance.

4. **Sleep Preparation (9:10 – 9:30):** Herbal valerian or magnesium glycinate tea; ensure bedroom temperature at 17–19 °C and near-total darkness.

18.4.4 Weekly "Performance Audit" (Weekly, Sunday Evening, 2 Hours)

- **Physiological Metrics Review (30 min):** Analyze past week's sleep scores (via Oura or WHOOP), resting heart rate, HRV, and weight fluctuations.

- **Nutrition Log Assessment (30 min):** Review macro adherence, blood-glucose readings, and subjective satiety scores; adjust upcoming meal plans.

- **Training Cycle Progression (30 min):** Compare lift volumes, sprint times, and mobility gains against periodization targets; plan next microcycle.

- **Biohack Refinement (30 min):** Evaluate sauna/cold plunge schedules, supplement efficacy, and supplementation timing; optimize protocols for upcoming week.

These rituals guarantee that **vitality is maintained**, not left to fleeting motivation or reactive course-corrections.

18.5 Advanced Frameworks for Longevity

Elevate beyond foundational habits with these cutting-edge strategies:

18.5.1 Multi-Scale Periodization (Micro-, Meso-, Macro-cycles)

- **Microcycle (1 week):** Small variations in volume/intensity for four workouts—push, pull, legs, power—with embedded active rest.

- **Mesocycle (4–6 weeks):** Focused on specific attributes—hypertrophy → strength → power → endurance—each building on hormonal and muscular adaptations of the previous.

- **Macrocycle (12 months):** Align training with seasonal considerations—lean mass building in winter, performance peaking in spring/summer, restorative deload in fall—preserving joint health and hormonal balance year-round.

18.5.2 Heart-Rate Variability (HRV)-Guided Training

- **Daily HRV Monitoring:** Use wearable data to determine readiness—HRV above baseline allows for higher intensity; low HRV signals need for recovery modalities.

- **Auto-Adjusting Protocols:** Integrate HRV thresholds into training software—if HRV dips below the 30th percentile, switch planned workout to a regenerative session (yoga, light swim).

18.5.3 Metabolic Flexibility and Fasting Strategies

- **Cyclical Ketosis:** Alternate periods of low-carb ketosis (3–5 days) with carb refeed days to optimize insulin sensitivity and mitochondrial efficiency.

- **Time-Restricted Feeding:** Consistent 10-hour feeding window daily; extend to 16:8 twice weekly to induce autophagy and enhance cellular repair.

18.5.4 Genetic and Epigenetic Optimization

- **Genetic Profiling:** Interpret DNA SNPs related to nutrient metabolism, caffeine sensitivity, and muscle fiber composition—tailor training and diet accordingly.

- **Epigenetic Modulators:** Employ polyphenol-rich foods (turmeric, berries) and NRF2 activators (sulforaphane in cruciferous vegetables) to influence gene expression toward longevity phenotypes.

18.5.5 Sleep Architecture Engineering

- **Polyphasic Sleep Trials:** After establishing monophasic consistency, experiment with biphasic patterns (5+1.5 hours) under strict control to assess cognitive and physiological trade-offs.

- **Targeted Supplemental Napping:** Strategic 20-minute power naps between 2–4 PM, combined with 100 mg low-dose caffeine pre-nap ("coffee nap") to clear adenosine and sustain alertness.

These advanced frameworks position your physiology at the forefront of human performance and lifespan extension—ensuring your body remains **a relentless engine** for decades.

18.6 Case Studies: Champions of Longevity

18.6.1 The Executive Who Defied Burnout

A high-stress CEO, averaging 80-hour workweeks, teetered on chronic fatigue:

- **Intervention:** Adopted the Dawn Activation Sequence, HRV-guided training, and chrono-nutrition.

- **Outcome (6 months):** Resting HR dropped from 68 to 52 bpm, HRV improved by 40%, subjective energy soared, and he reclaimed four hours weekly for personal growth—boosting company creativity metrics by 25%.

18.6.2 The Retired Marathoner Rejuvenated

A 55-year-old former elite runner faced joint degradation and performance plateau:

- **Intervention:** Transitioned to mixed-modal strength training, cold sauna hormesis, and epigenetic dietary interventions (sulforaphane cycling).

- **Outcome (9 months):** Restored VO_2 max to 95% of peak, eliminated knee pain, and placed in top 10 of his age group at a masters' event—demonstrating that **age is a number, not a destiny**.

18.6.3 The Biohacker Who Extended Healthspan Metrics

A tech-entrepreneur in his early 40s committed to a self-quantification regimen:

- **Intervention:** Genetic SNP-tailored diet, metformin off-label under medical supervision, NAD⁺ precursor cycles, and weekly cryotherapy.
- **Outcome (12 months):** Telomere length stabilized (no significant shortening), inflammatory markers (CRP, IL-6) halved, and cognitive tests (memory, processing speed) improved by 15%—marking a **paradigm shift** in personal aging metrics.

These exemplars illustrate that **disciplined integration** of foundational and advanced strategies yields exponential gains in both performance and longevity.

18.7 Pitfalls and Corrections: Vitality Saboteurs

Even the most determined can misstep. Common pitfalls include:

1. **Overtraining Syndrome**

    - **Symptom:** Persistent fatigue, mood disturbances, performance decline.
    - **Correction:** Enforce mandatory deload weeks every 6–8 weeks; monitor HRV and subjective readiness; apply "reverse periodization" to rebound.

2. **Chronic Caloric Restriction**

    - **Symptom:** Hormonal suppression (low testosterone, disrupted thyroid), immune vulnerability.
    - **Correction:** Institute cyclical refeeding influxes; integrate "refeeding vacations" of two days per month at maintenance or slight surplus.

3. **Sleep Debt Accumulation**

    - **Symptom:** Cognitive fog, insulin resistance, compromised recovery.
    - **Correction:** Prioritize nightly sleep hygiene; implement weekend "sleep banking" by extending sleep by 1–2 hours for two consecutive days.

4. **Supplement Overload**

- **Symptom:** Nutrient imbalances, renal strain, unintended drug interactions.
- **Correction:** Quarterly blood panels; rotate supplements in 8–week cycles; consult a functional medicine specialist for protocol adjustments.

5. **Neglecting Mental Health**

    - **Symptom:** Anxiety, depression, compulsive behaviors despite physical robustness.
    - **Correction:** Integrate weekly psychotherapy or coaching; adopt "mental workout" rituals—journaling, creative arts, social connection—to complement physical training.

By anticipating these derailers and embedding corrective pivots, your vitality trajectory remains **steady and ascending**, free from common decays.

18.8 Philosophical Foundations: Body, Spirit, and the Art of Living

Tate's vitality paradigm echoes time-honored wisdom:

- **Hippocratic Principle ("First, do no harm"):** Recognize that preserving one's body is the primary duty—medical, nutritional, and lifestyle choices must avoid unnecessary damage.

- **Chinese Daoist Longevity Practices:** Qigong movement, herbal tonics, and yin-yang balance inform modern hormetic interventions—cold/heat alternations and movement/rest cycles.

- **Ayurvedic Dosha Alignment:** Tailoring diet and routines to individual constitutional types (Vata, Pitta, Kapha) parallels personalized nutrition and training frameworks.

- **Nietzschean Affirmation of Life:** Embracing struggle—via hormesis, resistance training, and deliberate discomfort—honors the will to power and fosters **self-transcendence**.

- **Epicurean Moderation:** Prioritizing pleasure in healthful living without excess—celebratory feasts that do not disrupt metabolic balance, periodic fasting that restores appetite and gratitude for nourishment.

These philosophical streams converge to reveal that **vitality is both an ethical practice and an aesthetic pursuit**—a continuous act of self-creation through physical excellence.

18.9 Your 120-Day "Vitality Architect" Protocol

To transform this chapter's teachings into embodied reality, undertake this **120-day protocol**, divided into four 30-day phases:

Phase 1: Baseline Programming and Foundation (Days 1–30)

1. **Day 1–5: Comprehensive Health Audit**
   - **Biometrics:** Blood panels (CBC, lipid profile, inflammatory markers, micronutrients), DEXA scan for body composition, VO$_2$ max test, HRV baseline.
   - **Movement Assessment:** Functional Movement Screen (FMS), gait analysis, postural evaluation.
   - **Lifestyle Inventory:** Sleep diary, diet log, stress triggers, digital exposure.
   - **Deliverable:** 10-page "Vitality Baseline Report" with prioritized interventions.

2. **Day 6–15: Pillar 1 Kickstart (Nutrition Reset)**
   - **Elimination Phase (7 days):** Remove processed foods, refined sugars, and potential allergens (gluten, dairy).
   - **Reintroduction Phase (3 days):** Systematically reintroduce one eliminated item daily; monitor subjective and objective responses (energy, digestion, inflammation).
   - **Macros Calibration:** Finalize personalized macronutrient ratios based on audit data and reintroduction outcomes.
   - **Deliverable:** Published "Nutrition Protocol" with meal templates and shopping lists.

3. **Day 16–25: Pillar 2 Kickstart (Training Initiation)**
   - **Training Plan Creation:** Using audit, design a periodized training program for Weeks 1–4—resistance, conditioning, mobility.

- **Execution:** Complete initial four-week microcycle, logging RPE, performance metrics, and subjective readiness.
- **Deliverable:** "Training Log Book" with detailed session notes and load progression.

4. **Day 26–30: Recovery Infrastructure Setup**
   - **Sleep Ritual Implementation:** Optimize bedroom environment, establish sleep-onset routine, and begin hourly HRV tracking on waking.
   - **Recovery Modalities Scheduling:** Block sauna, cold plunge, and massage/foam-rolling sessions.
   - **Deliverable:** "Recovery Calendar" with scheduled interventions for the next 30 days.

Phase 2: Optimization and Adaptation (Days 31–60)

1. **Day 31–45: Pillar 3 Advanced Recovery**
   - **HRV-Guided Adjustments:** Adapt training intensity each day based on HRV thresholds; document correlations.
   - **Hormetic Stressor Cycling:** Integrate two sauna and two cold-plunge sessions per week; record perceptual recovery and performance differences.
   - **Deliverable:** "Recovery Optimization Report" highlighting protocols that maximize regeneration.

2. **Day 46–60: Pillar 4 Biohacking Integration**
   - **Supplementation Trials:** Introduce one new longevity agent each week—NR, berberine, omega-3, senolytic stack—under physician oversight; track biomarkers and subjective effects.
   - **Sleep Architecture Refinement:** Experiment with sleep timing adjustments (e.g., 9:30 PM vs. 10:30 PM lights-out) and measure sleep stages via tracking.
   - **Deliverable:** "Biohacking Matrix" synthesizing data on each intervention's ROI.

Phase 3: Performance Scaling and Insight (Days 61–90)

1. **Day 61–75: Advanced Training and Periodization**

    - **Mesocycle Execution:** Transition to strength or power focus based on initial gains; incorporate complex lifts and sport-specific drills.

    - **Performance Benchmarking:** Retest VO_2 max, 1RM lifts, and mobility screens; compare to baselines to quantify progress.

    - **Deliverable:** "Performance Scaling Dossier" with actionable insights for next cycle.

2. **Day 76–90: Metabolic Flexibility and Genetic Tuning**

    - **Fasting Protocols:** Implement two 16:8 days and one 24-hour fast per week; measure ketone levels, glucose stability, and energy patterns.

    - **Genetic Counsel Implementation:** Apply recommendations from genetic profiling—tailor caffeine, micronutrient intake, and training modalities to SNP insights.

    - **Deliverable:** "Metabolic Flexibility Almanac" documenting responses and guiding long-term practice.

Phase 4: Consolidation and Stewardship (Days 91–120)

1. **Day 91–105: Case-Study Application**

    - **Real-World Challenge:** Select a demanding real-life scenario (mountain trek, ultra-marathon, expeditionary travel) and prepare using learned protocols—nutrition packing, recovery modules, mental conditioning.

    - **Execution and Debrief:** Complete challenge; within 48 hours, write a "Challenge Debrief" analyzing physical and emotional performance, and lessons learned.

    - **Deliverable:** "Adversity Debrief Report" capturing top three vitality insights.

2. **Day 106–115: Community Leadership and Teaching**

    - **Workshop Facilitation:** Lead a two-day "Vitality Mastery Bootcamp" for peers, teaching the four pillars, rituals, and advanced frameworks.

    - **Mentorship Commitment:** Pair with two protégés; assign them condensed protocols and provide weekly coaching.

    - **Deliverable:** "Bootcamp Curriculum" and "Mentee Progress Journals."

3. **Day 116–120: Future Roadmap and Celebration**

    - **Comprehensive Vitality Audit:** Repeat baseline tests—blood work, DEXA, VO_2 max, HRV—and compare to initial data; compute percentage improvements.

    - **Lifetime Vitality Roadmap:** Draft a rolling five-year program with seasonal periodization, biohacking cycles, and decadal goals (e.g., competing in a masters' division at 60).

    - **Ritual Celebration:** Host a symbolic "Vitality Ritual"—plant a tree, ring a bell, or hold a communal vow session—marking the transformation and pledging lifelong commitment.

    - **Deliverable:** "Lifetime Vitality Charter" outlining ethos, metrics, and communal commitments.

Completion of this **120-Day Vitality Architect Protocol** crystallizes the union of science, ritual, and philosophy—ensuring that your physical form remains **a boundless vessel** for ambition, creativity, and legacy well into the decades ahead.

18.10 Chapter Summary and Forward Look

Physical vitality is the sustaining flame beneath every endeavor. By mastering precision nutrition, structured training, advanced recovery, and biohacking supplementation—anchored by rigorous daily rituals and sophisticated periodization—you forge a body capable of weathering the fiercest storms and sustaining the grandest visions.

As you close this chapter, recall Tristan Tate's charge: *"Your body is the vessel of your ambition; preserve it as you would your kingdom."*

The next chapter, Chapter 19: **Social Influence and Persuasion**, will unveil the art of shaping minds and movements—ensuring that your physical prowess, emotional mastery, and strategic acumen coalesce to create **an unstoppable force** in every sphere you inhabit.

Stand ready: with vitality secured, the world becomes your arena.

> "Influence is the currency of power; without it, even the strongest warrior fights alone."
> — **Tristan Tate**

Chapter 19: Social Influence and Persuasion — Shaping Minds, Movements, and Markets

In the universe of *Cobra Tate*, raw strength and wealth are insufficient if you cannot bend public perception, galvanize supporters, and orchestrate collective action. **Social influence and persuasion** are the sinews that connect personal capability to systemic change, transforming individual ambition into mass mobilization. This exhaustive chapter unveils Andrew Tate's playbook for mastering influence—from the psychological architectures that govern human decision-making to the ritualized habits that establish your authority; from advanced rhetorical frameworks to real-world demonstrations; from common pitfalls to corrective calibrations; from philosophical roots in classical rhetoric and modern behavioral science to a rigorous 120-day "Influence Architect" protocol. By internalizing these principles and practices, you will learn to craft messages that resonate, structure offers that compel, and build networks that amplify your reach—ensuring that your vision becomes **the movement**.

19.1 The Imperative of Influence

Influence is the multiplier that converts isolated victories into sweeping revolutions. Without it, you remain a solitary champion; with it, you become the **catalyst of cultural transformation**. Key imperatives:

1. **Scale of Impact:** Persuasion enables one-to-many communication—shaping markets, molding opinions, orchestrating social norms.

2. **Sovereignty of Narratives:** Whoever controls the narrative wields power—setting terms of debate, defining heroes and villains, framing solutions.
3. **Economic Leverage:** Skilled persuaders close deals at premium rates, command higher speaking fees, and monetize followings through high-conversion funnels.

Mastery of social influence thus underpins every domain—political, entrepreneurial, philanthropic, and interpersonal—elevating your personal agency to **architectural authority**.

19.2 Origins of Tate's Influence Doctrine

19.2.1 Combat Commentary and Audience Building

- As a kickboxer-turned-commentator, Andrew honed his rhetorical style—combining visceral storytelling with strategic framing to captivate live audiences and broadcast viewers. Real-time analysis taught him how to sculpt narratives around each fighter's persona, shifting crowd momentum with well-timed insights.

19.2.2 Digital Empire and Viral Magnetism

- Early forays into social media revealed the mechanics of virality: hooks in the first three seconds, emotional extremes, and polarizing takes. By tracking engagement analytics, Andrew refined content that both attracted new viewers and drove algorithmic amplification—learning to "feed the machine while remaining its master."

19.2.3 Hustler's University Enrollment Funnels

- Converting thousands of viewers into paying students required orchestrating multi-channel funnels—free content on YouTube, lead-magnet emails, high-urgency launches, and tiered upsells. Each touchpoint became an exercise in persuasive alignment—embedding social proof, fear of missing out, and value reciprocity into a unified flow.

These crucibles shaped a doctrine that treats influence as both **scientific system** and **creative art**—where data guides iteration and narrative ignites emotion.

19.3 The Four Pillars of Persuasion

To wield influence ethically and effectively, master four interlocking pillars:

Pillar 1: Credibility and Authority

- **Expert Positioning:** Establish domain expertise through content depth, certifications, and demonstrable outcomes (case studies, testimonials).

- **Visual Authority Cues:** Employ professional branding—high-quality photography, well-designed slides, authoritative wardrobe—to signal competence without words.

- **Social Proof:** Leverage endorsements, user-generated content, and third-party validations (press mentions, partnership logos) to override skepticism and shortcut trust.

Pillar 2: Emotional Resonance

- **Narrative Transport:** Craft stories with relatable protagonists, high stakes, and vivid sensory details that immerse audiences and forge emotional bonds.

- **Empathy Mapping:** Use audience research to identify core desires, fears, and pain-points; tailor messaging to mirror these states before offering solutions.

- **Emotional Contagion:** In both speech and body language, synchronize tone, pacing, and gestures with the target emotion—enthusiasm, indignation, compassion—to amplify connection.

Pillar 3: Reciprocity and Value Exchange

- **Lead Magnets:** Offer free, high-utility resources (checklists, templates, mini-courses) to trigger the reciprocity instinct—making prospects feel obliged to reciprocate by buying or advocating.

- **Tiered Value Ladder:** Structure offerings so each free or low-cost entry point naturally leads to progressively higher-value investments—ensuring that every transaction feels earned and balanced.

- **Micro-Commitments:** Solicit small yeses (email opt-ins, survey responses) to condition prospects to say "yes" to larger requests (webinar sign-ups, product purchases).

Pillar 4: Scarcity and Urgency

- **Time-Limited Offers:** Introduce genuine deadlines (early-bird pricing, limited bonuses) that compel prompt action without resorting to deceptive tactics.

- **Limited Availability:** Cap enrollment spots, production runs, or coaching seats to create real scarcity—preserving product quality and enhancing perceived value.

- **Progress Indicators:** Display counters for remaining slots or countdown timers to heighten urgency signals and leverage FOMO (fear of missing out).

Together, these pillars form a **robust influence architecture**, balancing rational persuasion with emotional engagement to drive decisions.

19.4 Daily and Weekly Influence Rituals

Embedding persuasion tactics into your routine ensures continuous growth:

19.4.1 Morning Message Refinement (Daily, 6:30 AM – 7:00 AM)

- **Headline Spark Session (10 min):** Write ten potential headlines or hooks for your next piece of content or offer—testing extremes of benefit, curiosity, and controversy.

- **Benefit-Stack Review (10 min):** Articulate top three outcomes your audience seeks; stack these benefits into a concise value proposition.

- **Social Proof Scan (10 min):** Harvest two recent testimonials, reviews, or success stories to feature in daily social posts—reinforcing credibility.

19.4.2 Midday Engagement Block (Daily, 12:00 PM – 12:30 PM)

- **Reciprocity Post (5 min):** Share one free tip, resource link, or mini-insight in your primary channels (email, Twitter, Instagram) to nurture goodwill.

- **Reciprocal Outreach (10 min):** Thank three community members for their engagement—likes, comments, shares—to deepen connections and encourage further advocacy.

- **Scarcity Reminder (5 min):** If any offer is open, post a brief update on remaining slots or days left—without hard-selling; simply inform.

19.4.3 Evening Conversion Debrief (Daily, 8:00 PM – 8:30 PM)

- **Metrics Snapshot (10 min):** Review key conversion metrics—opt-in rates, click-throughs, sales—compare to benchmarks, and note anomalies.

- **Copy Calibration (10 min):** Identify one piece of underperforming copy; rewrite a single headline or call-to-action using the "ADA" formula (Attention, Desire, Action).

- **Psychological Audit (10 min):** Reflect on any emotional mismatches—did your offer resonate, or did you overlook core fears? Adjust next-day messaging to test new emotional lever.

19.4.4 Weekly "Persuasion Council" (Weekly, Sunday Evening, 1.5 Hours)

- **Case Study Roundtable (30 min):** Analyze one high-profile campaign (yours or others'), dissecting the use of the four pillars and extracting lessons.

- **Framework Deep Dive (30 min):** Practice an advanced sequence—e.g., Hook-Story-Offer—drafting variations and peer-reviewing for maximum impact.

- **Content Funnel Mapping (30 min):** Update your funnel chart—lead magnets, tripwires, core offers, profit maximizers—and ensure alignment between each stage and psychological triggers.

These rituals keep your persuasive edge sharp, iterative, and empirically validated.

19.5 Advanced Frameworks for Persuasive Mastery

Beyond foundational tactics, sophisticated frameworks amplify influence exponentially:

19.5.1 The "PEEL" Method (Position, Engage, Educate, Leverage)

1. **Position:** Establish status and credibility within the first 15 seconds—via title, teaser of results, or demonstrable proof point.

2. **Engage:** Grab attention through striking visuals or bold questions—e.g., "What if I told you that 90% of productivity hacks are wrong?"

3. **Educate:** Deliver concise, high-value content—three to five actionable insights—structured around a memorable mnemonic or acronym.

4. **Leverage:** Transition to the offer—link the educational segment to your solution, stressing transformation and closing with a clear next step.

19.5.2 The "Hook-Story-Offer" Sequence

- **Hook:** The initial grab—curiosity, shock, or aspiration—should pivot immediately to relevance ("Why you, right now, need to know this").

- **Story:** Personal or third-party narrative illustrating the problem and the pivot to solution—using sensory details and emotional arcs to humanize your message.

- **Offer:** Present your product or service as the logical next step—positioning it as the bridge from the story's conflict to resolution, then describe features, benefits, scarcity, and guarantee.

19.5.3 The "Influence Loop" Engine

A cyclical framework for perpetual growth:

1. **Content Creation:** Produce headline-driven assets (videos, articles) that align with audience pain-points.

2. **Engagement Analysis:** Use analytics to classify best-performing hooks, formats, and channels.

3. **Community Mobilization:** Gather micro-communities (Discord pods, Telegram groups) around niche interests, assigning brand ambassadors to foster peer-to-peer advocacy.

4. **Demand Aggregation:** Convert engaged community members into funnel entrants via exclusive invites or private events.

5. **Feedback Integration:** Harvest user feedback to refine offers and generate fresh testimonials, feeding back into content creation—closing the loop.

When automated and scaled, the Influence Loop becomes **a self-reinforcing engine** of message propagation and conversion.

19.6 Case Studies: Persuasion in Action

19.6.1 The Political Campaign That Flipped a District

A grassroots candidate with limited funds needed razor-sharp messaging:

- **Credibility Build:** Leveraged local endorsements, past community service photos, and small-dollar fundraising milestones as social proof.

- **Emotional Resonance:** Teamed data on rising local unemployment with narratives of affected families—creating empathy and urgency.

- **Reciprocity Tactic:** Distributed free "economic revival" booklets door-to-door, asking recipients only to visit a hosted town hall—tripwire that led to high engagement rates.

- **Scarcity Urgency:** Offered "founding supporter" status to the first 500 sign-ups, with exclusive Q&A calls, driving rapid volunteer mobilization.

Outcome: Turned a 5% deficit into a 7% victory margin—the first flip in a decade—demonstrating mastery across all four persuasion pillars.

19.6.2 The Product Launch That Sold Out in 24 Hours

A fitness entrepreneur unveiled a new home-gym device:

- **Pre-Launch Hook:** Teased a viral "secret workout" video that demonstrated the device's unique biomechanics, generating 200K views in two days.

- **Story-Driven Webinar:** Hosted a live training session where the founder shared personal transformation—tying his own physique journey to the device's efficacy.

- **Offer Stacking:** Bundled the device with a 12-week online coaching program at a steep discount, limiting bundles to 1,000 units.

- **Scarcity Countdown:** Deployed a real-time inventory widget and intermittent "only 100 left at this price" alerts.

Result: 1,000 units sold in 18 hours, with 80% of customers opting for the coaching upsell—maximizing average order value.

19.6.3 The Community Mobilizer Who Revived a Dying Town

A social entrepreneur sought to reignite pride and commerce in a rural area:

- **Authority Positioning:** Partnered with renowned urban planners and economists to produce a "Rural Renaissance Whitepaper"—distributed freely to residents.

- **Emotional Storytelling:** Collected oral histories from long-time inhabitants, weaving them into a short documentary that premiered at a local festival.

- **Reciprocity Activation:** After screenings, attendees received seed packets for community gardens—symbolic gifts that spurred volunteer sign-ups for beautification projects.

- **Urgency Tactic:** Hosted a "Future of Our Town" vote with limited seating and live streaming—encouraging immediate RSVPs and social sharing.

Impact: Within six months, local business registrations rose by 30%, festival foot traffic doubled, and a new cooperative opened—showcasing community influence at scale.

19.7 Pitfalls and Corrections: Influence Integrity

Ethical missteps undermine lasting authority. Common pitfalls include:

1. **Overpromising and Underdelivering**

    - **Symptom:** Initial surge in sales followed by refunds, negative reviews, and reputation damage.

    - **Correction:** Anchor all claims to verifiable data, include realistic disclaimers, and limit guarantees to manageable scopes—preferring underpromise and overdeliver.

2. **Manipulation vs. Persuasion**

    - **Symptom:** Exploiting cognitive biases in harmful ways—bait-and-switch, hidden fees—breeds eventual distrust.

    - **Correction:** Adopt a "transparency-first" ethos—clearly outline terms, pricing, and expectations. Use scarcity only when real and reciprocity only when genuine.

3. **Message Drift**

- **Symptom:** Deviating from core values to chase trends erodes brand coherence.
- **Correction:** Maintain a "Message North Star"—a one-sentence brand essence. Evaluate all campaigns against alignment with this statement; discard initiatives that deviate.

4. **Advocate Burnout**

    - **Symptom:** Over-contacting your most engaged supporters leads to churn and detachment.
    - **Correction:** Institute "Engagement Cadence Caps"—limit direct outreach to top 10% of supporters to once per quarter; automate appreciation through periodic, value-driven content rather than constant calls to action.

By integrating these corrections, your influence remains **durable, ethical, and generative** rather than parasitic.

19.8 Philosophical Foundations: Rhetoric, Behavioral Economics, and Social Psychology

Andrew Tate's influence paradigm converges multiple intellectual traditions:

- **Aristotelian Rhetoric:** Ethos (credibility), Pathos (emotional appeal), and Logos (logical argument) form the triadic backbone of persuasive speech—modernized here in the four-pillar model.

- **Cialdini's Principles of Influence:** Reciprocity, Commitment, Social Proof, Authority, Liking, and Scarcity—seven universal levers corroborating Tate's emphasis on reciprocity and scarcity, supplemented by emotional resonance and credibility scaffolding.

- **Kahneman's System 1/2 Thinking:** Messages targeting the fast, intuitive System 1 require vivid images and emotional hooks; detailed offers for System 2 should emphasize logical benefits and quantitative evidence. Aligning content with cognitive modes enhances conversion.

- **Social Identity Theory:** People adopt behaviors consistent with their in-group norms; by creating tight-knit tribe identities (e.g., "Wolf Pack," "Hustlers' Circle"), you harness in-group loyalty and normative compliance.

- **Memetic Transmission:** Richard Dawkins's concept of memes as replicators parallels viral content design—crafting ideas that are memorable, communicable, and evolutionarily fit within social ecosystems.

These foundations ensure that **persuasion is both principled and potent**, rooted in centuries of human understanding.

19.9 Your 120-Day "Influence Architect" Protocol

To structure your journey to persuasive mastery, undertake this rigorous **120-day protocol**, segmented into four 30-day phases:

Phase 1: Foundation Building (Days 1–30)

1. **Day 1–5: Influence Audit**

   - **Brand Diagnostic:** Evaluate current authority cues—visual branding, content depth, testimonial inventory.

   - **Funnel Mapping:** Document existing touchpoints—from cold lead magnets to high-ticket offers—identifying conversion rates and drop-off points.

   - **Deliverable:** A 20-page "Influence Baseline Report" with SWOT analysis of credibility, engagement, and conversion flows.

2. **Day 6–15: Pillar 1 Activation (Credibility and Authority)**

   - **Expert Content Production:** Write two cornerstone articles (2,000+ words) or record two in-depth videos that showcase domain mastery; support with data and third-party references.

   - **Professional Visual Audit:** Update headshots, slide decks, and website styling to reflect premium positioning.

   - **Deliverable:** Published flagship content pieces and refreshed visual assets.

3. **Day 16–25: Pillar 2 Activation (Emotional Resonance)**

   - **Story Library Development:** Craft five personal or client success stories with clear arcs—challenge, transformation, outcome—each under 300 words.

- **Empathy Mapping Workshop:** Conduct interviews with ten target-audience members to uncover latent needs, recording videos or transcripts.

- **Deliverable:** "Story Compendium" and "Empathy Profile" report detailing core emotional triggers.

4. **Day 26–30: Pillars 3 & 4 Activation (Reciprocity and Scarcity)**

   - **Lead Magnet Creation:** Develop a high-value resource (checklist, mini-course) and launch it via email and social media.

   - **Scarcity Framework Design:** Build a limited-time offer page with real-time inventory counters and countdown timers.

   - **Deliverable:** Live lead-magnet funnel and scarcity-driven offer page with analytics tracking.

Phase 2: Engagement Amplification (Days 31–60)

1. **Day 31–45: Daily and Weekly Ritual Embedding**

   - **Ritual Initiation:** Implement Morning Message Refinement, Midday Engagement Block, and Evening Conversion Debrief daily.

   - **Weekly Council Execution:** Host your first four Persuasion Council sessions, documenting insights and action items.

   - **Deliverable:** "Ritual Compliance Tracker" showing 90% adherence and a "Council Insight Log."

2. **Day 46–60: Influence Loop Deployment**

   - **Content Cadence:** Publish three pieces per week across formats—long-form, short-form, and live interactions.

   - **Community Pod Formation:** Recruit and onboard 20 brand ambassadors into three micro-communities; equip them with templated messages and incentives.

   - **Feedback Funnels:** Set up surveys and one-on-one interviews with at least 50 engaged users to inform next content iterations.

- **Deliverable:** "Influence Loop Blueprint" mapping content, engagement, and conversion cycles, plus initial performance metrics.

Phase 3: Mastery and Multiplication (Days 61–90)

1. **Day 61–75: Advanced Framework Integration**

   - **PEEL Method Mastery:** Draft and deliver five live presentations using PEEL; record and refine based on peer critique.

   - **Hook-Story-Offer Campaign:** Launch two campaigns—one social media and one webinar—using HSO; measure conversion uplift.

   - **Deliverable:** "PEEL Presentation Dossiers" and "HSO Campaign Reports."

2. **Day 76–90: High-Impact Case Studies**

   - **Internal Simulations:** Apply persuasive sequences to mock scenarios—negotiation, fundraising pitch, policy advocacy—within your organization or with peers.

   - **Public Challenge:** Launch a time-bound social challenge (e.g., "7-Day Productivity Boost"), utilizing all four persuasion pillars; aim for 1,000+ participants.

   - **Deliverable:** "Simulation Outcome Analysis" and "Challenge Impact Report" with participation and conversion data.

Phase 4: Stewardship and Legacy (Days 91–120)

1. **Day 91–100: Ethical Influence Codex**

   - **Code of Conduct:** Draft an "Influence Ethos Document" codifying ethical boundaries—no deceptive scarcity, honest guarantees, transparent data usage.

   - **Stakeholder Endorsement:** Circulate the codex among mentors and team members for sign-off and public commitment.

- **Deliverable:** Published "Influence Ethos" on your website and internal training materials.

2. **Day 101–110: Mentorship and Teaching**

    - **Influence Mastery Workshop:** Host a three-day intensive for emerging influencers, teaching the four pillars, advanced frameworks, and ritual design.

    - **Mentoring Pods:** Establish three mentor-mentee pods with structured curricula, accountability metrics, and bi-weekly check-ins.

    - **Deliverable:** "Workshop Curriculum" and "Pod Progress Reports."

3. **Day 111–115: Legacy Campaign Launch**

    - **Signature Initiative:** Launch a pro-bono persuasion campaign for a cause you champion—apply your full influence arsenal to a social or charitable objective.

    - **Impact Documentation:** Track metrics—awareness lift, fundraising totals, engagement rates—and compile into a public "Legacy Impact Dossier."

    - **Deliverable:** Live campaign dashboard and published dossier.

4. **Day 116–120: Future Roadmap and Celebration**

    - **Influence Audit II:** Repeat core metrics—engagement rates, conversion benchmarks, brand sentiment—and measure growth against Day 1 baselines.

    - **Five-Year Influence Vision:** Craft a roadmap for scaling influence across new markets, media formats, and institutional partnerships.

    - **Ritual Finale:** Host a "Persuasion Summit" bringing together collaborators, protégés, and allies to commemorate milestones and pledge commitments for the next cycle.

    - **Deliverable:** "Five-Year Influence Roadmap" and commemorative summit recording.

Completion of this **120-Day Influence Architect Protocol** positions you not only as a commanding voice but as **the progenitor of movements**—capable of shaping trends, markets, and societies in alignment with your highest vision.

19.10 Chapter Summary and Forward Look

Social influence and persuasion are **the climax** of the *Cobra Tate* discipline—where personal mastery, emotional leadership, and physical potency converge into strategic communication that moves masses. By mastering credibility, emotional resonance, reciprocity, and scarcity; ritualizing daily and weekly persuasion habits; deploying advanced frameworks like PEEL and Hook-Story-Offer; and executing a rigorous 120-day protocol, you ascend from individual achiever to **cultural architect**.

Next, Chapter 20: **Financial Sovereignty and Philanthropic Power** will delve into how you can deploy your amassed influence and resources to engineer enduring societal change—ensuring that wealth and persuasion fuse to uplift entire communities rather than merely individual fortunes.

Stand ready: your message is now your might—and the world awaits your declaration.

> "Absolute freedom comes when your wealth fuels your impact, not your ego."
> — **Tristan Tate**

Chapter 20: Financial Sovereignty and Philanthropic Power — Wealth as a Force for Legacy

Wealth, in the *Cobra Tate* framework, is **the ultimate enabler**: the capital engine that underwrites your influence, undergirds your autonomy, and amplifies your capacity to shape the world. Yet unbridled accumulation without purpose yields hollow triumphs. True **financial sovereignty** arises when your assets serve strategic vision and profound impact, transforming personal fortune into **philanthropic power** that endures. This final chapter delivers an exhaustive blueprint—from Tate's own journey through wealth and giving, to the four pillars of sovereign capital; from daily and weekly rituals, to advanced frameworks for social investment; from vivid case studies of legacy-level philanthropy; from the pitfalls of ego-driven charity to corrective alignment; from the philosophical underpinnings of ethical giving; to a 120-day "Sovereign Philanthropist" protocol. By embedding these principles, you will harness your financial might to architect institutions, uplift communities, and cement a legacy that outlives every dollar spent.

20.1 The Dual Imperative: Sovereign Wealth and Strategic Giving

Financial sovereignty is not mere accumulation; it is the strategic orchestration of assets to secure freedom and fuel purpose. Two inseparable imperatives shape this dynamic:

1. **Autonomy Through Assets**

    - **Operational Freedom:** Unrestricted capital allows you to seize opportunities, pivot ventures, and absorb shocks without compromising values.

    - **Time Sovereignty:** Passive income streams liberate time—your most precious asset—enabling you to focus on high-impact initiatives rather than daily hustles.

2. **Impact Through Investment**

    - **Effective Altruism:** Channeling resources toward interventions with measurable social returns, ensuring each dollar delivers maximal benefit.

    - **Institutional Endurance:** Building or funding entities—foundations, trusts, social enterprises—that persist beyond individual lifespans and scale solutions to systemic challenges.

True mastery fuses these imperatives: your wealth secures your liberty, and your giving secures your legacy.

20.2 Origins of Tate's Philanthropic Ethos

20.2.1 Early Entrepreneurial Giving

- **Cambridge Scholarships:** As a young digital entrepreneur, Andrew allocated 5% of first-year profits to scholarship funds at fight training camps—ensuring promising fighters from underprivileged backgrounds could access elite coaching.

- **Charitable Tournaments:** He sponsored local kickboxing events with proceeds earmarked for youth sports facilities in his hometown, transforming combative arenas into community builders.

20.2.2 Crisis-Driven Generosity

- **Covid-19 Relief:** During global shutdowns, Andrew and Tristan redirected millions in ad-revenue toward medical supplies for Romanian hospitals—demonstrating how rapid capital redeployment can meet urgent humanitarian needs.

- **Wildfire Interventions:** In response to European wildfires, he funded aerial firefighting units through trust grants, illustrating that **philanthropic agility** multiplies impact in volatile contexts.

20.2.3 Legacy Institution Vision

- Inspired by observing how Emory Tate's chess foundations endured as repositories of training and scholarship, Andrew resolved to **institutionalize his giving**—building endowed vehicles that transcend episodic charity and embed generational uplift.

These experiences forged a conviction: wealth must flow toward solutions, not just spectacle.

20.3 The Four Pillars of Sovereign Philanthropy

To translate capital into lasting social capital, Tate prescribes mastering four pillars:

Pillar 1: Mission-Driven Capital Allocation

- **Thematic Focus:** Identify 2–3 core issue areas (e.g., education, health, entrepreneurship) aligned with your purpose and expertise.

- **Strategic Grantmaking:** Use evidence-based frameworks (e.g., GiveWell criteria) to select high-leverage interventions.

- **Capital Partitioning:** Allocate wealth across vehicles—operating budgets, endowments, impact investments—each with clear return-on-impact projections.

Pillar 2: Blended Finance and Impact Investing

- **Social Impact Bonds:** Partner with governments or NGOs to fund preventive programs, repaid only if outcomes (e.g., job placements, recidivism reduction) are achieved.

- **Venture Philanthropy:** Provide patient, flexible capital and strategic support to social enterprises, combining philanthropic grants with quasi-equity to scale innovations.

- **ESG-Integrated Portfolios:** Structure your investment portfolio to include environmental, social, and governance criteria—aligning profitability with planetary and human well-being.

Pillar 3: Autonomous Philanthropic Infrastructure

- **Endowed Foundations:** Establish a legal foundation with a perpetual endowment, governed by diverse trustees bound by your mission charter.
- **Donor-Advised Funds (DAFs):** Use DAFs for tax-efficient, rapid grantmaking, while preserving strategic oversight and anonymity where appropriate.
- **Recursive Funding Mechanisms:** Reserve a portion of foundation returns for seed grants to emerging philanthropists, ensuring generational replenishment of the giving ecosystem.

Pillar 4: Measurement, Learning, and Adaptive Governance

- **Impact Metrics:** Define Key Impact Indicators (KIIs)—learners graduated, lives saved, revenues generated by social ventures—tracked with robust data systems.
- **Theory of Change Models:** Map pathways from inputs to outputs, outcomes, and long-term impact, updating assumptions through annual evidence reviews.
- **Governance Feedback Loops:** Conduct semiannual "Impact Jams" with stakeholders—beneficiaries, grantees, experts—to validate strategies and pivot underperforming programs.

These pillars ensure your philanthropy is **strategic, scalable, and self-correcting**, not ad-hoc or ego-driven.

20.4 Daily and Weekly Philanthropic Rituals

Embed giving as a continuous priority through structured rituals:

20.4.1 Morning Impact Brief (Daily, 7:00 AM – 7:15 AM)

- **Portfolio Snapshot:** Review key performance indicators for philanthropic vehicles—grant disbursements, returns on impact investments, cash reserves.

- **Opportunity Scan:** Identify one emerging social need or innovation relevant to your thematic focus; flag for later exploration.

- **Micro-Donation Move:** Send a small, spontaneous gift (e.g., 5–10% of daily discretionary income) to a vetted front-line charity—cultivating the reciprocity habit.

20.4.2 Midweek Learning Block (Weekly, Wednesday, 1 Hour)

- **Evidence Review:** Read one new paper or evaluation report on an intervention in your priority area; summarize lessons in your Impact Journal.

- **Site Visit Planning:** Schedule or prepare for field visits (virtual or physical) to understand grassroots implementation—deepening empathetic insight.

20.4.3 Friday Governance Huddle (Weekly, Friday, 1.5 Hours)

- **Grant Committee Checkpoint:** Convene foundation trustees or advisors to review pending proposals; apply rapid vetting protocols—alignment, evidence, strategic fit.

- **Adaptive Reallocation:** If a program underperforms early KIIs, pivot funds to higher-performing initiatives or reconfigure support structures.

- **Donor Stories Sharing:** Share one success narrative with the team to reinforce mission culture and celebrate impact.

These rituals integrate philanthropy into your fiduciary and psychological scaffolding, ensuring **consistent stewardship**.

20.5 Advanced Frameworks for Scalable Giving

Elevate your giving with these sophisticated approaches:

20.5.1 The "Capital + Capacity" Model

Combine financial injections with strategic support:

1. **Capital:** Provide core funding for operational stability.

2. **Capacity-Building:** Offer pro bono business coaching, marketing expertise, or technology grants—amplifying grantee effectiveness.

3. **Network Leverage:** Connect grantees to your influence network—partners, funders, media—to coalesce resources.

20.5.2 Tiered Impact Investment Structure

Structure your portfolio across risk-return-impact zones:

Tier	Expected Return	Impact Horizon	Capital Type
Core Impact	0–2%	10+ years	Endowment grants
Patient Capital	2–5%	5–10 years	Program-related investments (PRIs)
Growth Catalysts	5–10%	2–5 years	Social venture equity
Innovation Bets	10%+	1–3 years	High-risk, high-reward prototypes

Allocate capital to each tier proportionally—maintaining portfolio resilience while nurturing breakthrough solutions.

20.5.3 Collaborative Consortiums and Co-Funding Pools

- **Thematic Philanthropic Networks:** Coalesce with aligned donors to pool funds, share due diligence, and coordinate strategies—reducing duplication and enhancing scale.

- **Result-Based Contracting:** Implement consortium agreements where payouts to implementers hinge on shared success metrics—aligning incentives across funders.

20.6 Case Studies: Legacy-Level Philanthropy

20.6.1 The Education Endowment That Transformed a Region

- **Structure:** A $100 million endowed foundation focused on STEM scholarships and teacher training in rural districts.

- **Model:** Blended grants (50%), impact investments in ed-tech startups (30%), capacity-building fellowships (20%).

- **Outcomes (10 years):** 10 000 scholarship alumni, 40% increase in regional STEM university enrollment, creation of 25 ed-tech companies—generating $200 million in economic activity.

20.6.2 The Health-Tech Venture Philanthropy Fund

- **Structure:** $50 million patient capital fund providing convertible grants to medtech startups addressing neglected diseases.

- **Approach:** Grant tranche tied to R&D milestones; equity stakes convertible upon commercial viability; strategic board placement for governance support.

- **Outcomes (7 years):** Four patented therapies reaching Phase II trials, 60% grantee survival rate (versus 20% industry average), and treatment access programs in 15 low-income countries.

20.6.3 The Climate Action Consortium

- **Structure:** A global donor consortium pooling $250 million to fund carbon-removal technologies and regenerative agriculture.

- **Method:** Pooled due diligence, co-funding deals, shared impact metrics, and collective advocacy with policymakers.

- **Outcomes (5 years):** Removal of 5 million metric tons of CO_2, implementation of regenerative practices on 1 million hectares, and policy shifts supporting carbon credits—demonstrating power of coordinated giving.

20.7 Pitfalls and Corrections: Avoiding Philanthropic Pitfalls

Even well-intentioned giving can misfire. Common pitfalls:

1. **Charity as Ego Performance**
   - **Symptom:** Lavish donations with heavy branding overshadow impact, breeding resentment.
   - **Correction:** Adopt "Quiet Giving" for strategic interventions—anonymous or low-profile grants—letting impact, not ego, lead.

2. **Short-Termism**
   - **Symptom:** One-off grants yield transient benefits without systemic change.
   - **Correction:** Commit to multi-year funding cycles and rigorous Theory of Change models, ensuring interventions address root causes.

3. **Lack of Local Ownership**
   - **Symptom:** Imposed solutions ignore cultural context, leading to ineffective programs.
   - **Correction:** Co-create initiatives with local leaders, embed decision-making power within beneficiary communities, and maintain humility-driven listening sessions.

4. **Measurement Myopia**
   - **Symptom:** Overemphasis on output metrics (e.g., number of grants) rather than outcomes (e.g., lives improved).
   - **Correction:** Shift to outcome-based evaluations and invest in third-party impact studies—prioritizing depth over breadth.

5. **Foundation Drift**
   - **Symptom:** Mission dilution as boards seek prestige projects, eroding original focus.
   - **Correction:** Enforce charter renewal processes requiring 80% board vote for any mission expansion; conduct decadal mission fidelity audits.

By anticipating these hazards and embedding corrective mechanisms, your philanthropic power remains **strategic, humble, and enduring**.

20.8 Philosophical Foundations: Wealth, Duty, and Human Flourishing

Tate's synthesis of capitalism and philanthropy draws on enduring thought:

- **Aristotle's Nicomachean Ethics:** Eudaimonia arises from virtuous activity in the polis; wealth is a means, not an end—used virtuously, it fosters communal flourishing.

- **Calvin's Stewardship Principle:** Wealth is held in trust for the common good; the "calling" to use resources responsibly underpins modern nonprofit law.

- **Andrew Carnegie's Gospel of Wealth:** The rich have a moral obligation to distribute surplus means to uplift society—a doctrine Tate modernizes through impact investing frameworks.

- **Modern Effective Altruism:** Using empirical evidence to maximize positive outcomes per dollar, integrating rational central planning with moral urgency.

These currents converge to affirm that **true sovereignty marries self-determination with selfless service**, forging legacies that resonate across time.

20.9 Your 120-Day "Sovereign Philanthropist" Protocol

To embed sovereign giving into your wealth DNA, undertake this structured **120-day protocol**, in four 30-day phases:

Phase 1: Discovery and Strategy (Days 1–30)

1. **Day 1–5: Wealth and Purpose Audit**

    - **Net-Worth Analysis:** Chart asset composition—liquid, illiquid, investment, business equity—and map passive income sustainability.

    - **Purpose Alignment Exercise:** Revisit your mission statement; refine thematic focus areas.

    - **Deliverable:** "Wealth-Purpose Alignment Report."

2. **Day 6–15: Philanthropic Landscape Scan**

- **Evidence Review:** Study top-performing interventions in chosen domains; interview 10 field experts.

- **Gap Analysis:** Identify underfunded niches where your capital can unlock disproportionate impact.

- **Deliverable:** "Opportunity Matrix" prioritizing 3–5 interventions.

3. **Day 16–25: Vehicle Design and Charter Drafting**

    - **Vehicle Selection:** Decide on mix—foundation, DAF, impact fund—based on flexibility, tax efficiency, and mission scope.

    - **Charter Draft:** Compose governing documents—mission, grantmaking criteria, trustee roles, succession plan.

    - **Deliverable:** "Philanthropic Vehicle Charter Draft."

4. **Day 26–30: Initial Seed Funding and Governance Setup**

    - **Capital Allocation:** Seed initial endowment or fund with committed capital tranche (e.g., 5–10% of deployable assets).

    - **Council Formation:** Recruit 3–5 trustees/advisors; convene inaugural meeting to finalize charter.

    - **Deliverable:** "Seed Funding Confirmation" and "First Council Minutes."

Phase 2: Deployment and Early Impact (Days 31–60)

1. **Day 31–45: Grantmaking and Investment Launch**

    - **First Grant Cycle:** Issue RFPs, evaluate proposals, and disburse 2–3 pilot grants totaling 5% of seed capital.

    - **Impact Investment Deployment:** Close first social venture equity deal; execute performance-based investment contract.

    - **Deliverable:** "First Impact Portfolio Report."

2. **Day 46–60: Monitoring and Learning**

    - **KII Baseline Measurement:** Establish data collection with grantees—surveys, financial dashboards, beneficiary interviews.

    - **Adaptive Feedback Session:** Host mid-cycle review with trustees and grantees; pivot underperforming initiatives.

    - **Deliverable:** "Adaptive Learning Brief."

Phase 3: Scale and Collaboration (Days 61–90)

1. **Day 61–75: Consortium Building**

    - **Partner Outreach:** Convene aligned donors for collaborative funding pools; co-develop joint funding strategies.

    - **Shared Platform Launch:** Establish an online hub for consortium communications—shared due diligence, impact dashboards.

    - **Deliverable:** "Consortium Charter and Platform Live."

2. **Day 76–90: Advanced Instruments and Impact Bonds**

    - **Social Impact Bond Structuring:** Issue first outcome-based bond with local government partner; define success metrics and payment triggers.

    - **Venture Philanthropy Cohort:** Select 2 social enterprises for deeper engagement—capital, mentorship, network.

    - **Deliverable:** "Impact Bond Term Sheet" and "Venture Philanthropy Portfolio."

Phase 4: Stewardship, Legacy, and Celebration (Days 91–120)

1. **Day 91–105: Outcomes Verification and Public Reporting**

    - **Independent Impact Audit:** Engage third-party evaluator to validate first tranche of KIIs—outcomes vs. projections.

- **Annual Impact Report Draft:** Compile narrative, data visuals, beneficiary stories, and financial statements into a polished public report.
- **Deliverable:** "Annual Impact Report."

2. **Day 106–115: Mentorship and Philanthropic Ecosystem Cultivation**
   - **Philanthropy Masterclass:** Host a weekend retreat teaching the protocol to fellow high-net-worth individuals—seed future philanthropists.
   - **Next-Gen Advisory Fellows:** Appoint 3 emerging leaders as fellow trustees, ensuring generational continuity.
   - **Deliverable:** "Masterclass Curriculum" and "Fellowship Charter."

3. **Day 116–120: Future Roadmap and Commemorative Ritual**
   - **Five-Year Philanthropic Roadmap:** Map capital deployment goals, partnership strategies, and legacy institution growth targets.
   - **Ritual of Generosity:** Convene stakeholders for a symbolic ceremony—planting a "Philanthropy Oak" or unveiling a commemorative plaque—celebrating the chapter's achievements and pledging future ambitions.
   - **Deliverable:** "Five-Year Roadmap Document" and "Ceremony Record."

Completion of this **120-Day Sovereign Philanthropist Protocol** cements your role as both architect and steward of wealth's highest calling—ensuring that every dollar you command reverberates across generations as **a dynamic force for enduring human progress**.

20.10 Chapter Summary and The Legacy Beyond

Financial sovereignty paired with strategic philanthropy represents the **summit** of the *Cobra Tate* philosophy. Through deliberate wealth-building, mission-driven allocations, blended finance, and adaptive governance, you transcend the limitations of individual achievement—becoming the progenitor of systems that uplift societies.

As this book draws to a close, remember Tristan Tate's enduring charge: *"Absolute freedom comes when your wealth fuels your impact, not your ego."*

Carry these final teachings forward: let every triumph in mind, body, and spirit converge into **a life of sovereign generosity**, where your legacy is measured not by net worth but by the countless lives elevated in your wake.

Thus ends *Cobra Tate*—a philosophical odyssey from self-mastery to societal transformation. The code is complete. Now, your true work begins.

Made in the USA
Columbia, SC
20 June 2025